FROM SIL

TO

PARTICIPATION

From Silence to Participation

An Insider's View of Liturgical Renewal

BERNARD BOTTE
Translated by John Sullivan, O.C.D.

The Pastoral Press
Washington, D.C.

From Silence to Participation: An Insider's View of Liturgical Renewal is a translation of *Le mouvement liturgique: Témoignage et souvenirs* © Desclée et Cie, Paris, 1973.

ISBN: 0-912405-54-6

The Pastoral Press
225 Sheridan Street, NW
Washington, D.C. 20011
(202) 723-1254

© Copyright 1988, The Pastoral Press

The Pastoral Press is the publications division of the National Association of Pastoral Musicians, a membership organization of musicians and clergy dedicated to fostering the art of musical liturgy.

Printed in the United States of America

Dom Bernard Botte, O.S.B.
1893-1980

Contents

Translator's Foreword

SAINT JUSTIN MARTYR HAS LEFT US a description of an ancient eucharistic celebration in his *First Apology* which says the assembled people listened to the "recollections" of the apostles. Historical research confirms that those "recollections" were the texts of the New Testament proclaimed to the liturgical assembly for their joy, comfort, and nourishment on life's journey. In the present book we can read descriptions of contemporary events, all within our century, that are offered to us also in the form of recollections from someone who was an eyewitness to the ebb and flow of a great movement.

This series of reflections by the Belgian Benedictine monk, Bernard Botte (1893-1980), presents us with a fascinating account of the major stages of the twentieth century liturgical movement from its inception in the first decade of our "age of anxiety" through the completion of several revised rites of the Roman Catholic Church in the early 1970s. Dom Botte had the good fortune of being associated with those we call liturgical pioneers all along the arc of the forward progress of liturgical renewal. He shared in their uncertainties, their disappointments, but also in their dogged fidelity to the hard task of reminding the church that the liturgy is a great spiritual fountainhead and resource when it functions as it ought.

Although he interacted with the hierarchical centers of power which eventually embraced the vision of those pioneers, Botte tells us what happened not from an official perspective but "from below," as it were. He therefore speaks more of dreams than of documents; and he sounds more like a storyteller frequently relying on instructive and delightful anecdotes than a professor of history surgically explaining events long since gone. Even though he admitted to this translator that he did not prepare his book by speaking into a microphone in oral history fashion, he has successfully captured an almost one-on-one tone in his narrative, one which easily draws the reader into the vision he shared with his coworkers in the movement.

To publish this translation at the end of the 1980s is to suggest at least two things: there is room for continued efforts toward deepening our understanding of liturgy's central place in the life of the church; we can benefit from other firsthand accounts of the people who have been working for liturgical renewal all along. Collections of the official documents of liturgical revision are now readily available, but an understanding of their spirit often depends on an appreciation of the dreams of those experts who were responsible for drafting them. It is to be hoped that many more sets of recollections will be written and published so that the ongoing quest for living liturgy can be guided by the inspiring life stories of other dedicated individuals like Dom Botte. True, new tasks await new generations, just as new tools, new methods, and new problems are now at hand. Still, we can benefit from hearing how those who preceded us confronted the crises of their day and went on to leave a living heritage for the future.

John Sullivan, O.C.D.

Introduction

THERE ARE TWO kinds of writers. The first have a calling to write, are driven to write out of personal need: they feel they have a message to convey to others and want to do so as well as they possibly can. The second kind are those who write out of necessity, the sort of people who are led by chance to write something or other and who have been asked to continue at it. Once they have been caught up in the machinery, they can no longer escape. I think I belong to the company of these hard working laborers. When I look over my own bibliography, everything I see was requested by some publisher, magazine editor, or congress organizer. On my own I never would have thought of undertaking an edition of the *Apostolic Tradition* of Saint Hippolytus, still less of writing an article on "Hippolytus (Canons of)" between "Hippocrates" and "Hippopotamus" in the very scholarly *Encyclopedia Britannica*.

So now, when it's time to rest, I am seated in front of my typewriter to write down things no one has requested from me. Could it be that at this late date I've discovered I have a message to pass on to the world, and that I don't want to die before I've done so? I'm not that naive. Or is it that I can't stop myself because of the momentum I've built up, just like the character in *Zazie dans le metro* who, after coming down the circular stairway of the Eiffel Tower, kept on going around in circles outside the exit? This could be, but I would like to justify my plan all the same, and this is what I've found.

I was an eyewitness to the beginnings of the liturgical movement and, doubtless, am the last witness still around. For quite a long time I was personally involved and I knew most of the men who influenced the movement. Perhaps twenty years from now historians will feel the desire to ask me about it, but I won't be here to reply. Therefore, I am going to provide the answers ahead of time. In other words, I'm complying with an order in advance.

If the readers aren't satisfied with this explanation, they are free to suggest another. In all events, don't look for any sensational revelations here. I have no secret documents to make public. The events I will recall are known, and all I can add are the details. Still, what I'd like to do above all else is to place these events in a light different from that of historians, because historians work in archives, that is, with written documents. The people they describe are only names to them. To me, however, they are living persons who deserve more than oblivion.

1

Starting Point

The author describes in detail several liturgies as they were celebrated near the turn of this century. Just as we do not *enjoy* the sight of fossils in a museum, one can hardly enjoy reading Botte's account of these antiquated ways of "saying Mass." Still, they are instructive (and quaintly humorous) period pieces. Many people will recognize one or another aspect of his sketches.

Botte pays particular attention to those "in charge of the liturgy," the priests: their lifestyle, training, presiding and preaching while celebrating. Obvious inadequacies and harmful assumptions then current led some individuals to react and thereby take the first steps of the twentieth century liturgical movement. For Botte, its early focal point and center was the Benedictine Abbey of Mont César he joined in 1912 in the central Belgian university town of Louvain not far from Brussels. This abbey was founded from Maredsous Abbey, another Belgian Benedictine monastery which benefited from the nineteenth century stirrings of liturgical interest in the German Beuronese congregation. (Tr.)

T O UNDERSTAND A MOVEMENT you have to know its starting point. How was the liturgy carried out at the beginning of the twentieth century? Young people today evidently cannot imagine this; and people who are a little older—those fifty and over—would be off the mark if they relied on their childhood memories, since many things have changed in twenty years. We have to go back to the very first years of the century, to the time I entered high school. To be sure, I wasn't one of those child martyrs who put up with high school as if it were a period of forced labor and who remain scarred by it for the rest of their days. Accordingly, my criticisms are not motivated by bitterness. I loved my old high school and I had a good time there. Nor was I a precocious child whose esthetic sense would have been offended by the literary and musical barrenness of the songs we had to sing. As innocent as could be, I sang full blast along with the others: "O Jesus, you enflame me with celestial ecstasies," or "Fly, fly, angels of prayer." My criticisms are retroactive. With hindsight I will try to take another look at the facts and understand them.

Every morning at eight o'clock there was a Mass in the students' chapel. Actually, it was a large study hall with a row of pews placed on either side of a central aisle. Up front there was only one altar in a little apse located between two sacristies. Mass was said by an old, more or less voiceless, priest—even in the first row the only thing you'd hear was a murmur. The group rose for the gospel, but nobody dreamed of telling us which gospel it was. We didn't even know what saint's feast it was or which deceased persons were being prayed for at the Masses said with black vestments. The people's missal did not exist. You could lose yourself in any prayerbook at all, but we were pulled out of our drowsiness from time to time by the recitation of a few decades of the rosary, or by the singing of either a Latin motet or a French hymn. The only time we would pray with the priest was after Mass when the celebrant, kneeling at the foot of the altar, recited the three "Hail Marys" with the "Hail, Holy Queen" and the prayers prescribed by Leo XIII. Receiving communion at this Mass was out of the question. For that matter, no one at the time seemed to notice a relationship between the Mass and communion.

Things weren't much better in the two parishes of my home town. There were some sung Masses, but they were a dialogue between the clergy and the cleric-organist. The people remained quiet and passive, doing whatever each one liked, saying the rosary or losing oneself in *The Most Beautiful Prayers of Saint Alphonsus Liguori* or *The Imitation of Christ*. As for communion, it was distributed before Mass, after Mass, or in the middle of Mass, but never at the moment indicated by the liturgy. The schedule was the determining factor: communion was distributed every fifteen minutes. When Mass began on the hour you were sure to see, as the clock struck a quarter past, a priest in a surplice come out of the sacristy, rush to the altar, and interrupt the celebrant in order to take a ciborium out of the tabernacle. The celebrant then was allowed to continue the Mass until he was disturbed once again by the ciborium being returned to the tabernacle. When one of my sisters asked the advice of the dean of the upper end of Charleroi, Monsignor Lalieu (a doctor of theology and an author of a book on the Mass), about the best time to receive communion, he recommended she receive before Mass and then offer Mass in thanksgiving for communion. This sounds strange to us, but we ought to keep in mind the ideas then current. Mass was no longer the prayer of the Christian community. The clergy prayed entirely in place of and in the name of the community. As a result, the faithful were only remotely involved and paid attention to their own personal devotion. Communion appeared to be a private devotion without any special link to the Mass.

So, the clergy were in charge of the liturgy. How did they carry it out? In general, with dignity, by observing the rubrics. Nonetheless, there was something strange. Almost all of them seemed to be in a terrible hurry and to suffer from a striking speech impediment. Even without a knowledge of Latin you couldn't help noticing that they stammered and mumbled a good number of syllables; and those acquainted with Latin made some delightful discoveries. A priest I knew placed Saint Michael the Archangel and Saint John the Baptist so close together in the *Confiteor* that he created a new saint, *beato Michaeli Baptistae* [Saint Michael the Baptist]. The same priest regularly proclaimed the following formula before communion: *Ecce Agnus Dei, ecce peccata mundi* [Behold the Lamb of God, behold the sins of the world]. All this apparently did not scandalize anyone, provided it didn't go to extremes; but the floundering around added nothing to the beauty of the ceremonies.

In the meantime, the faithful prayed as best they could, and on their own. The only times they prayed together was when the rosary was recited aloud or when hymns were sung. Much has been said mocking these hymns; and it's true that several were ridiculous. It would perhaps be amusing to compile an anthology of this literature, but to tear them apart is too easy, and, really, it's unjust. Thousands of simple people have found nourishment for their piety in those naive stanzas. By singing them together they were able to experience a moment when they were a fraternal community of believers and not an anonymous crowd like travelers brought together by chance in the lobby of a train station. The scandal doesn't lie in Christians singing these hymns, but rather in their not having anything else to nourish their faith and piety. For we must admit that preaching was at its lowest level in those days.

I'd be reproaching myself if I were to discredit a generation of priests who always seemed respectable to me. Almost all the priests I knew when I was young were holy and zealous. They lived in simplicity and very close to the people, especially in the working-class parishes. The only luxury you might have begrudged them was their wine cellar. Still, wine wasn't that much of a luxury in Belgium during those prosperous years. For the clergy this was a question of a long-standing tradition of hospitality. When a pastor had his confreres visit him for Forty Hours or a deanery meeting, he was supposed to provide a good meal with wine. In my diocese there was a limit to be observed which was guided by the rule *una minus*, that is, if ten persons were present, they were allowed only nine bottles. Aside from these fraternal meals, most priests lived modestly and proved themselves charitable and generous. People didn't stop themselves from laughing about the clergy's whims and idiosyncrasies, but the priests were respected. There were some rare exceptions, but these only confirmed the rule. The priests I knew when I was young did not at all resemble the caricatures seen in *L'assiette au beurre*. They were good priests, conscientious about their responsibilities. How to explain, then, that things had reached a point which seems unbearable to us today? We must keep in mind the kind of education they received.

A majority of priests had six years of humanities studies in Greek and Latin before entering the seminary. Then they had two years of philosophy and at least three years of theology. How good was their theological training?

Dogmatic theology was the foundation of their studies. The different tracts had been formed gradually, flowing out of polemics with the Protestants, the Jansenists, and modern philosophers. After Vatican I the theologians seemed to have grown a bit drowsy, and their research was directed toward disputes among the different schools, disputes of no general interest. All this was summarized into skeleton-like manuals made up of a series of theses supposedly proven by sketchy arguments taken from Scripture, the Fathers, and the Councils. Everything was horribly dry and off-balance. It is hard to see how this could have been useful for preaching, except to check whether you were falling into heresy.

A corrective role might reasonably have been expected from the courses of Holy Scripture. Unfortunately this was not the case at all, and the situation here was even worse. Catholic exegesis had taken a radically negative position vis-à-vis Protestant or independent biblical criticism. The Scripture courses were accordingly turned into courses of apologetics. You had to refute the adversaries and then resolve difficulties that sometimes proved to be imaginary. A case in point was the "biblical hare." Not long ago someone gave me an incredulous look because I mentioned that this hare had troubled the sleep of many an exegete. The Bible classifies the hare as a ruminating animal, something which is a definite error to naturalists. How could you explain that the Holy Spirit had so poorly inspired Moses? Those interested in the problem will find an attempted solution in the *Dictionnaire apologétique de la foi catholique* of Père A. d'Alès, and they'll see that I'm not making anything up. The Scripture textbooks were loaded with similar problems of the same kind: Moses' authorship of the Pentateuch, creation in six days, universal extension of the flood, Joshua's stopping the sun, the concordance and disagreement of the Gospels, and many similar questions. With such introductions given by the textbooks, you were held back from going any further since you didn't have any time or desire left to read the biblical text. To form a good judgment about the level of Catholic biblical studies at this time you need only read through Vigouroux's *Dictionnaire de la Bible.* One day I was gullible enough to look through it for an article on grace. None existed, but I did find out that the wide variety of greases mentioned in the Bible was very well documented. The Bible was regarded as a venerable but somewhat bothersome monument. It often came under attack; you did well to protect it by speaking about it as little as possible. Such was the reaction that seemed to have caused this apologetical teaching. Once in a while a passage of Scripture would be cited to prove a point, and sermons would even begin with a biblical quotation, but these bits of isolated texts didn't have any great effect. They sounded as if they had been pulled out of some "Preacher's Thesaurus" instead of from the Bible itself, because the same ones always showed up—and with the same mistakes. This allowed a meticulous Jesuit to write a book on the biblical misinterpretations of preachers.

As for moral theology and canon law, they were taught with confessional practice in mind. The manuals of theory were matched by collections of cases of conscience. This teaching, I believe, was effective, but it was primarily a morality of sin, that is, a negative morality. One silly story told of the following dialogue: "What did the pastor preach about"? "About sin." "What did he say about it"? "He's against it." It's true that sermons were frequently "contra," and this was not without its usefulness, but you would have liked them more often to be "pro."

Finally, the liturgy. Here you have to know the exact meaning of the term "liturgy" as then taught. When you study the Mass or the sacraments, you can do so from three points of view: you can make a synthesis of the truths which the church proposes to us about them; you can also describe in detail the church's prescribed rites; finally, you can study the liturgical prayers which tradition has passed on to us. The first approach was the object of dogmatic theology. The second belonged to the course in liturgy. The third aspect was entirely neglected. Liturgy, then, meant "rubrics." This misunderstanding long survived in some people's minds. As a result, in 1921 or 1922 I heard Canon A. De Meyer, professor at the University of Louvain, declare in his history class that the people should be left to their popular devotions, and that they'd never be interested in the rubrics of the missal. I don't know what brought on this definitive judgment against the liturgical movement—probably the presence of a few Benedictines in the room. But this provides an exact idea of what the word "liturgy" evoked in the mind of a university professor. Liturgy, consequently, was the ceremonial part of worship emptied of its real content. The goal was to prepare clerics for correctly carrying out ritual acts, and this was very good. Only it is regretable that no one ever thought of explaining the liturgical texts and showing the spiritual riches they contain. From the way these texts were read it was apparent that most priests devoted only indirect attention to their meaning. The texts were neither food for clerical piety nor a source for sermons.

These are the reasons, I think, for the poor preaching at the beginning of the twentieth century. The clergy were poorly prepared for the ministry of the word of God by such substandard teaching. Neither the classes of theology, nor those of Scripture, nor those of the liturgy offered material for preaching. The clergy had nothing to say except for moralizing sermons, the kind they themselves had heard over and over again. They preached out of duty, because it was prescribed, just as they observed the rubrics. I remember the remark of an old Jesuit priest for whom I always had great esteem: "Preaching is a bore: you repeat the same thing all the time and that bores everybody." Priests no longer believed in preaching.

Perhaps you might be surprised that, in speaking of the liturgical movement, I should stop to consider at such length the question of preaching. The reason is that preaching is part of the liturgy. As far back as you go in tradition, there has never been liturgy without the proclamation and explanation of the word of God. To dream of a liturgy that is self-sufficient would be utopian. It would be contrary to all tradition, whether in the East or in the West. The great bishops like Saint John Chrysostom and Saint Augustine believed in their duty of inspiring the congregation by their word which explained the Scriptures. It would also be contrary to the most elementary psychology: on every civil holiday someone gives a speech explaining the meaning of the day and expressing the sentiments of everyone present.

Undoubtedly the priests of the nineteenth century were not responsible for the veil which the use of Latin had hung between the altar and the nave, but they did nothing to break through this curtain. Their preaching could have made the people partially aware of the riches contained in the biblical readings and liturgical prayers, but the clergy themselves were ignorant of these riches, and that is their excuse. Regardless of where we place the responsibility, the harm was profound. Not only were the rites carried out in a hurry, but the faithful had nothing more to sustain their faith than substitute nourishment, and they lost the meaning of certain values. The Apostolate of Prayer once used the following debatable slogan: "Go to Mass on Sunday out of duty, but go to Mass on Friday out of love." This is the heart of the matter. The Mass was a personal obligation for each Christian, imposed arbitrarily by a positive law of the church. Forgotten was the idea that Sunday Mass is the central meeting of the people of God where all the faithful come to hear together the word of God and to be nourished by the bread of life. We had to wait for Pius X to remind us that the eucharist is not a reward for the perfect souls who sought a "me-alone-with-Jesus" encounter, but the normal food of Christians who want to live their faith. Left to themselves, the faithful became more and more isolated in a religious individualism and narrow moralism whose ideal was to have each one work on personal salvation by avoiding mortal sin.

The liturgical movement was born out of a reaction to this situation. The first indication I had of the movement was the publication of *La vie liturgique*. It always contained the Ordinary of the Mass as well as monthly inserts that gave the Proper of the Sunday Mass with a small supplement. Here I read that some study days would be held at the Abbey of Mont César. I already knew of the Abbey of Maredsous and, since I was thinking of becoming a Benedictine, I decided to take advantage of this opportunity to see this other monastery which I had never heard of. This is why, on a beautiful day in August 1910, I got off the train at Louvain, climbed for the first time the hill on the road to Malines, and rang the bell of the monastery where I was to spend the rest of my life.

2

Birth of the Movement

An appeal made at a meeting attended by both lay and ordained Catholics, not a document from some ecclesiastical
organism or authority, is Botte's choice as the starting point
for the contemporay liturgical movement. He takes the
Malines Catholic Congress of 1909 as the initial marker for
the trail we are still on. The Congress was a national gathering for reflection and planning about all facets of Catholic life,
and at it Dom Lambert Beauduin, also a monk of Mont César,
issued a manifesto calling for "the active participation of the
faithful in the liturgy of the church" through "understanding
the liturgical texts and singing together by the faithful."

Dom Beauduin was a threefold pioneer in the Catholic
Church of our century who contributed to the spread of
sound liturgical practices, ecclesiology, and ecumenism.
Botte tells us of his early life story and of how he pursued his
dream of seeing liturgy function as a true source of the life of
the church. Of note for the assimilation of the liturgical movement in the United States is that the Collegeville Benedictines
made a translation of Beauduin's little treatise *Liturgy the Life
of the Church,* the first volume of their "Popular Liturgical Library" series in 1926. (Tr.)

H ISTORIANS OF THE LITURGICAL MOVEMENT unanimously set the
date of its birth on the day that Dom Lambert Beauduin
gave his report about the participation of the faithful in
Christian worship at the Malines Congress in 1909. You might ask
whether it is improper to draw up a birth certificate for a movement of ideas the same way as for a newborn baby. The ideas proposed by Dom Beauduin weren't revolutionary, and he himself
denied being an innovator. On the contrary, he depended on
tradition and frequently invoked the words of Pius X on the participation of Christians in the holy mysteries as the indispensable
source of life. Clearly Beauduin's ideas came from people before
him. But if it's a question of the movement properly so called, that
is, of action, that's something else again. Forgive me for this rather
unscholastic definition, but you have a movement when things
are stirring. If the report of Dom Beauduin had remained an
academic discourse buried among the official acts of a congress,
there wouldn't have been a movement. The latter began only on
the day when ideas became translated into action by concrete initiatives and when a sustained effort toward changing things had
been launched. There's no doubting this point. When you trace
the progress of the liturgical movement across the different countries of Europe and the Americas you notice that it is the same
movement which continues on: not simply because the initiative
of Dom Beauduin was the first in time, but because there are
always traces of a positive influence. It was indeed from Mont
César that the liturgical movement started out.

When I first arrived at Mont César I was sure of the importance
of what was happening and, in fact, everyone was aware of it. I
found myself in a completely new monastery, still unfinished,
with a small community. The abbey had been founded in 1899 by
Maredsous. There were seven professed religious who came from
Maredsous, five others since the foundation, a novice, and five
lay brothers.

The abbot, Père Robert de Kerchove d'Exaerde, was the image
of an old Flemish gentleman, courteous and a little distant. His
early years were spent living in a castle or traveling abroad. Nothing apparently had prepared him for monastic life. One day he
told us about the origin of his vocation. He had decided, at a certain point, that it was time to settle down. He made up his mind
and left to present his case to the parents, who lived on the coast,
of the girl he had chosen. Just as he was about to ring the doorbell

he had a change of mind and said to himself: "Let's think this over a bit more." He then took a walk along the seashore, and it was the ebb and flow of the waves which suggested to him stern reflections on the fragility of the things of this world. So, he decided to dedicate himself entirely to God. He did this seriously, just as he did everything. It was he who had been assigned by the abbot of Maredsous, Dom Hildebrand de Hemptine, to get the foundation ready by obtaining the different properties covering the hill of Mont César and to oversee the construction of the first buildings. He arrived at the Louvain train station on 13 May, 1899 along with the group of founding religious, and they went to the abbey in procession, led by the cross. He was an honest and conscientious man, courageous as well.

The prior was Dom Eugene Vandeur who succeeded Dom Columba Marmion when he became abbot of Maredsous. Young, smiling, and likeable, he was still little known, but he quickly became a much sought-after spiritual director. He wrote some books on spirituality, one of which was entitled *The Christian Virgin in Her Family.* The book had a flyer that read: "This book aims to make young girls virile, to make them women . . . " Unfortunately the good Father let himself get involved in the foundation of a new congregation of women which brought a series of troubles his way. He died at Maredsous, not so long ago, at ninety. The last time I saw him, I thought I saw again his youthful and welcoming smile. Could it have been an illusion?

The subprior was Dom Bruno Destrée, the brother of the Socialist deputy of Charleroi. Complete baldness made his profile, which resembled that of the Saxe-Coburg family, much sharper. He took up writing very young. He was the Olivier-Georges-Destrée who was a member of the *La Jeune Belgique* group. Art and poetry had brought him back to the faith. His memories of his trips to Italy were radiant, not only for the light and landscapes he admired, but also for the country's saints and mystics. He kept on writing poetry, and during my novitiate I learned to type by copying his poems. He also had been influenced by the theology courses of Dom Columba Marmion. However, he used to make a distinction. Dom Marmion's classes were much better when he hadn't the time to prepare them. As a matter of fact, when he did prepare them, he'd go off into subtle distinctions which bothered the poet in Dom Bruno.

Dom Hilaire Delaet was a holy man, but his piety was a little too showy. A journalist pointed out that during the processional entrance of the monks into Louvain one of the monks was shaking his rosary a great deal. This was certainly Dom Hilaire. His tendencies toward scrupulosity rendered him unfit for certain tasks. The good priest could scarcely do more than pray for his confreres, and this he did with wholehearted fervor.

Dom Léon Cools was a priest of the Malines diocese before entering Maredsous. He trained the lay brothers and did some apostolic work in the neighborhood around the monastery. He had a passion for politics. When his interest slackened during recreation, you only had to mention aloud the word "liberal" to rouse him and see his eyes glint menacingly.

Dom Ildephonse Dirkx was cantor and bursar. As cantor he succeeded in training the choir whose singing was very good in spite of the small number of voices. As bursar he managed his general task, but his job included directing the farm—an area in which he was incompetent. In fact, he bought a head of beef from which he never got the slightest drop of milk—and for a good reason. He knew a bit about archeology and put together a rather large photo collection. Later on he was to go over to the Byzantine Rite and follow Dom Beauduin to Amay. There he would grow a beautiful red beard.

Dom Willibrord van Nierop was the first to be professed at Mont César. He was a robust Dutchman with a full voice, and was the joy of the community for his naiveté and his quaint way of speaking. I confess I sometimes took advantage of his simplicity but, all the same, we were good friends.

Dom Albert de Meester de Betzenbroek was a delayed vocation. He completed his law studies, then worked for a while at the Ravenstein Museum in Brussels. He looked a bit like a disillusioned aristocrat. Until the end, Dom Albert had a very special sense of humor. When he was over ninety his health required constant treatment. Since an infirmarian couldn't be found, the prior decided to get a nurse. He wanted to prepare Dom Albert to accept this infraction of the canonical rules and said to him: "Père Albert, I have taken the responsibility of letting a woman into your cell." Père Albert then smiled slyly and said "Finally!" Beneath his sometimes nonchalant exterior he had a heart always ready to be helpful and to accept all assignments. For a long time he was subprior, then prior. What he enjoyed most, though, was growing flowers in the garden. Since his death you hardly see flowers there any more.

Dom Michel Darras, on the other hand, was an early vocation. A long time ago Maredsous used to accept very young aspirants for the monastic life and had them do their studies in the humanities with the other students of the secondary school. Dom Michel had been one of these young oblates. He always retained a certain gift of youthfulness and admirably succeeded in teaching the fundamentals of music and Gregorian Chant to children from six to ten years of age. When he felt they were ready enough, he introduced them to the director of the choir and didn't concern himself with them any longer. And the children, once allowed into the choir, no longer paid any attention to him. He would smile and, with the most perfect degree of detachment, begin all over with a new generation. You'd see him, well past eighty, entering the church and followed by a bunch of tiny children whose restlessness he calmed with unflagging patience.

Dom Benoît Bourgois was the Good Samaritan of the community. He was infirmarian for many years and took care of the sick with admirable dedication. When he was replaced as the community's infirmarian by someone younger, he found sick people to take care of in their homes. All bent over, he'd be seen walking around town with his shopping bag in which he piled everything he had found to care for his friends. Among those I'm speaking of here, he was the last to pass on.

Dom Idesbald Van Houtrive acquired a reputation as a spiritual writer by a series of books with peace as their theme. They were well received and even gained more success than he desired. One day he received the spiritual writings of a French religious whose beatification process was being opened. This sister had revelations from the Holy Spirit, and she used to say without any apologies: "Today the Holy Spirit told me . . . " Now, to the utter surprise of Dom Idesbald, what followed was taken from his own works. This wasn't the only time he had been plagiarized. A Spanish book depended for a good half of its pages on a translation of a book by Dom Idesbald. But the author was a Benedictine, and we were all from the same family. You don't take a confrere to court any more than you'd file charges against the Holy Spirit.

Dom Joseph Kreps is the most picturesque figure in this picture gallery. He belongs to Louvain's folklore. Back in 1910 he played the organ and continued to do so till his death. He became a very great organist. But he's too rich a character and, since I have to come back to him later on, I won't say any more about him for the time being.

Dom Lambert Beauduin was the last of the professed members of the abbey. When I first made his acquaintance in 1910 he was still a young man. His good nature, kindness, and cordiality won me over. Forty years later I had my nephew (a young chemical engineer) take me by car to Chevetogne. We saw Dom Lambert together. Then I left my nephew and went to meet another priest. When I came back, they were the best of friends. Afterwards my nephew told me that he had never met anyone so likeable. Dom Beauduin was that way. By the end of a half-hour's conversation you had the impression you were his best friend. I had looked for an epithet that could best characterize him. I didn't find it in the dictionary but in a title of Chesterton: *Supervivant.* He overflowed with life and made it spring up all around him.

As a priest of the diocese of Liège, Dom Beauduin spent a few years in the young congregation of the Labor Chaplains. Why did he leave them? I can only repeat what he once told me: "By entering a congregation of religious I thought I'd find a life a little more recollected than in the diocesan clergy, but it's completely the opposite." He had experienced a form of the apostolate that wasn't suited to him because he tended to spread himself too thin in it. He then experienced monastic life and found his balance. But he also found it in another form of apostolate, one which a monastic community can exercise as a source of spiritual life. When he began working for the unity of the churches, he was most careful to found a monastic community that would be a center of ecumenism. He remained faithful to his monastic ideal throughout all his life. If he lived for several years outside the monastery, this wasn't his fault. It is well-known that he was made to leave Amay-Chevetogne, and at that time was exiled from Belgium. I don't have to judge or defend him here. As far as I'm concerned, I think he had commited a *faux pas* that did not deserve permanent exile. But the shadow of the exile order still paralyzed those who relied on his return, and he was not able to go back to Mont César. When the prior of Chevetogne, Dom Thomas Becket, had to courage to let it pass, Dom Lambert joyfully returned to take his place in the community he had founded. There was no bitterness in him, no recriminations over the past; no vanity, either, over the fact that his work had succeeded. He never worked for himself, solely for the church. He didn't expect any reward. He lived happily with his brothers. Was his death to be the occasion for public recognition of his work and accomplishments? Could it be possible that the last document which future historians would find in the Vatican Archives concerning him was a sentence of banishment? Only in 1959 did this old man, soon to die, receive a public token of John XXIII's appreciation, and still, it almost did not happen in time because of a stupid diplomatic incident which I will mention later on.

You might wonder, perhaps, whether it was really necessary to page through this family album in order to understand the origins of the liturgical movement. I sincerely believe it was because people frequently have the wrong idea.

Some imagine that Dom Beauduin, when he launched the liturgical movement, was backed by a strong team of "Benedictine scholars" to help him and supply him with information. In fact, this was not the case at all. Certainly his confreres accomplished valuable services for him, but none of them had any special competence. Among the older men, only Dom Vandeur had solid theological training. The younger men—well, they had just finished their studies in theology and had not received any special training.

As a result, you're tempted to draw another conclusion: the liturgical movement is Dom Beauduin and him alone. This is equally wrong. Dom Beauduin, himself, had no special training. The education he received was the same as the one given in seminaries and, as I said earlier, it was rather meager. The liturgy course was a course in rubrics. Nor did he have time to teach himself during his ministry as associate pastor or during his stay with the Labor Chaplains. In fact, Dom Lambert discovered the liturgy, if I may put it that way, only during his novitiate: in the celebration of the divine office and the Mass with this young, small community. The books and studies came later. But, at the beginning, there was a life experience together with confreres who, although not specialists, believed in what they were doing and did it well.

The services rendered by the community to Dom Lambert were modest yet indispensable: copying out texts, correcting proofs, making up parcels or licking stamps doesn't require genius, but they do show good will and dedication. All Dom Lambert's projects would have been without substance unless humble people had generously accepted these menial tasks. Furthermore, two of the most effective collaborators of Dom Lambert were two lay brothers: Brother Landoald de Waeghe, a robust farmer from the district around Ghent, a man full of common sense, and porter of the monastery; Brother Antoine Piérard, from northern France, who did not persevere in the monastic vocation. Without detracting from the merits of Dom Beauduin in the least, one must say that the liturgical movement—at its inception—was the work of the whole abbey.

Looking at things from a distance, I've often told myself that Dom Beauduin's undertaking was imprudent. How did he dare, with so few means and so limited a personal background, to launch such a movement, and how did he bring it off? There are other cases of a holy lack of prudence in the church's history, just like bad checks which Divine Providence has covered. Those who want to be certain of success before they start out generally don't get much done. Dom Beauduin dared because he believed in what he was doing. He thought it was much better to act than to complain about a situation which was far from bright.

If Dom Beauduin met with success, it was because his undertaking answered a real need felt on several levels. One of the best supporters of *La vie liturgique* was a young Jesuit, Père Joseph Wyns, who collected two hundred subscriptions at the high school of Charleroi. As monitor he was obliged to perch himself each morning on a small platform in front of the students and contemplate their total boredom during Mass. Many parish priests asked themselves whether, by boring people, they might end up chasing them away. I'm not saying they had grasped well the entire meaning of the liturgical movement. Keeping people from boredom and from running away was not the ultimate goal of the movement, but it was certainly part of it. This led to opening a dialogue with the clergy and supplementing their training. Moreover, the faithful were happy not to be treated as illiterates unable to understand what their pastors said or did. Dom Beauduin, who had experience in parish ministry, felt that the moment was favorable for his undertaking.

Another circumstance helped his plan along. After the efforts of Dom Guéranger liturgists, like the theologians, had grown drowsy and ended up in a tangle of rubrics. Now a new generation of scholars was emerging: in France, Louis Duchesne, Fernand Cabrol, Pierre Batiffol, and Pierre de Puniet; in England, Edmund Bishop and Henry Albert Wilson. Dom Beauduin would be able to rely upon their work. He himself wasn't a scholar. He hadn't done any university studies and, besides, he didn't have time to do organized research. But he knew how to draw from this reawakening of liturgical studies everything useful for inculcating the meaning and value of the church's worship. He did not aim at the academic world but at pastors. The movement began with a simple, practical production: *La vie liturgique.* It would continue with other achievements, especially by the magazine *Questions liturgiques et paroissiales* and with the study weeks.

3

La Belle Epoque

In the years immediately preceding the outbreak of World War I the organization of liturgical renewal started taking shape in Belgium. Publications began, along with liturgical weeks aimed at creating in the priest participants an appreciation for the place of liturgy in their ministry. Efforts to have similar liturgical weeks in the United States were underway in the late 1920s, proving the appeal they had for American liturgical pioneers.

Botte points out that what is now called "consciousness raising" was the main goal at that time, and not re-forming liturgical practices. Changes in ritual would have to come later on, but the then current efforts at creating renewed esteem for the liturgy were not merely cosmetic either, for this was "not a question of pastoral tactics but of theological truth." One instance of a stir caused by anti-liturgical piety—emanating from a Jesuit editor in France—is placed on the record by Botte in this chapter. (Tr.)

A PERIOD IS NEVER BEAUTIFUL for everyone, nor in every respect. The years preceding World War I have never stopped exerting a certain fascinating influence on the people of my generation who talk about them just as Adam and Eve must have spoken about the garden from which they were expelled. Still, not everything was rosy, especially for the Catholic Church. At this time Modernism was raging and, along with and as a reaction to it, a conservatism that conducted "witch hunts." It was said that Canon Ladeuze, Rector Magnificus of Louvain University, was kept from being appointed apostolic protonotary because of an article on the *Magnificat* that threw doubt on the Blessed Virgin's composition of this canticle on the basis of textual criticism that seemed to suggest Elizabeth's authorship. When his appointment finally arrived, Canon Cauchie sent the following telegram to the Rector: *Magnificat.* The liturgy was obviously less dangerous territory than biblical criticism; and if the liturgical movement had its nay-sayers, they stood within the bounds of polite argument. As far as I know, there weren't any calumnious denunciations or dishonest maneuverings. The movement had much freedom to evolve, and polemics only enhanced interest in it. From my point of view, I believe this was its beautiful period. Someone will perhaps say that I labor under an illusion here because this was the time of my own youth. I believe, rather, it was the young days of the movement itself, with their enthusiasm and boldness. In a few years the movement would set down such strong roots that, once the storm was over, the tree would blossom again.

At any rate, I will now speak about this period. As mentioned previously, I first visited Mont César in 1910. I made some other quick visits there, but I entered the monastery for good only in 1912. I think I can use this term "for good" after sixty years of perseverance.

There were new faces. In the novitiate there were a Portugese and three Belgians. Only one of the latter persevered in monastic life: he was Dom Hadelin Roland who recently died in the Abbey of Saint-André after a half-century of apostolate in the bush in Katanga.

But what was a Portugese doing at Mont César? Benedictine life had just about died out in Portugal at the beginning of the century, but survivors had asked the help of the Beuron Congregation (to which we belonged), and they had recruited some young men who desired to live the monastic life. Unfortunately, a revolution broke out in Portugal and the religious were expelled. The young novices were received by several monasteries of the Congregation. The one adopted by Mont César was a small, swarthy fellow, stocky and energetic. He received all his training at the Abbey and became a full-fledged member of the community. We would have liked to have kept him in Louvain, but after the war he left to restore monastic life in his country, where he created a liturgical movement which is still quite lively. When he left Louvain I drove him to the train. I've never seen him again. His name was Antonio Coelho.

During the school year the community was enlarged by the presence of some choir monks of Maredsous who came to do their theology studies, and by some priests who were faculty members along with Dom Vandeur and Dom Beauduin. Among the students was one who is well known to liturgists: Dom Mercenier. He had completed his class work in classical philology at the university and was finishing his theology. He was already fascinated by the Byzantine liturgy, and when he said the office alone he recited the psalms in Greek. Afterwards he was professor for a few years at the Abbey College of Maredsous where his students were delighted by his touch of naiveté and by his beautiful Walloon accent of the Sambre-et-Meuse district. Later on he joined Dom Beauduin at Amay where he dropped the name of the patron saint given him when he entered the novitiate, that is, Saint Feuillen, and placed himself under the protection of an unquestionably eastern saint, Saint Euthymius. Dom Mercenier is well-known for his translations of the Byzantine offices. He has been criticized on occasion for excessively literal renderings. The following invocation to Christ has been attributed to him: "Pitiful philanthropist, incomprehensible son of a Father without principle." But I've never found this passage, and I suspect it was just a joke.

Several German priests were also studying at the university. One of them became the great liturgist, Dom Cunibert Mohlberg. He finished his doctorate in moral-historical studies under the guidance of Canon Cauchie. Dom Mohlberg has always been appreciative of his teachers at Louvain and takes pleasure in showing respect for them. He has produced good work. Unfortunately, at one point he adopted a dictatorial style and had his work done by collaborators whom he treated like slaves.

But let's return to Mont César. As I said earlier, the first thing produced was *La vie liturgique* which each month published the Sunday Masses for the dioceses of Belgium. This publication lasted five years, from 1909 to 1913. It was then replaced by a *Missel dominical*, edited by the Vromant publishing house of Brussels.

This was a handy little book, with a bright and attractive layout. Meanwhile, another publication, *Questions liturgiques et paroissiales*, had begun. A bimonthly, the first issue appeared at the beginning of 1911, but an editorial decision soon had the volumes coincide with the beginning of the liturgical year so that each of the following volumes spanned two years: 1911-1912, 1912-1913, 1913-1914. The last issue published before World War I was dated July 1914. Reading these four volumes impresses one with the number and diversity of the topics treated. A parish priest today would probably say they aren't practical enough. But you have to understand what Dom Beauduin wanted to do.

First notice the adjective "parish" ("paroissiales"). It seems a little dated today and we'd replace it with the word "pastoral." Dom Beauduin insisted greatly on this. Much later I proposed he drop the adjective, but he protested. He didn't want the magazine to become a technical publication reserved for specialists. He really wanted its audience to be the parish clergy, those who were in contact with the people. It was a question of reestablishing contact between the altar and the nave in order to make the liturgy an act of a living community. The initiative couldn't come from the faithful. The priest had to go to the people; and if something was to change, the priests had to be spoken to so they'd be convinced.

On the other hand, Dom Beauduin didn't intend to give the clergy practical recipes. The priests didn't need that. What was needed was a change of spirit to make them understand that the liturgy is not a simple ritual mechanism but a source of life for them and for their people. Once they were convinced, the priests themselves would definitely find a way to put their convictions into practice. They had to be given the information they didn't obtain in the seminary. Today we'd call it continuing education.

We should also note that the liturgical movement, at its beginning, was not a reformist movement. Dom Beauduin knew very well that there were some cobwebs on that venerable monument called liturgy. One day or another these would have to be dusted away. But he did not consider this as essential and, at any rate, it was not his business. Under Pius X a reform began in Rome. It can be credited with the restoration of Gregorian Chant, renewed esteem for the Proper of the Season and the reform of the Roman Breviary. The reform stopped with the death of Pius X, but there were hopes at the time that it would continue. Dom Beauduin had a completely different point of view. He regarded the liturgy as a traditional given which we first of all had to try to understand. This was wise and prudent. To understand liturgy you had to turn to history, to archeology, to philology. That way you'd uncover the true meaning of the rites and texts, be enabled to distinguish essentials from accidentals, and have access to the spirit of the liturgy. Once the true meaning of things was uncovered, what was obsolete would automatically disappear. Once we realized what the Easter Vigil was, we'd hardly be able to keep it at six o'clock in the morning. But to propose a reform in 1910 would have seemed dangerously utopian, and Dom Beauduin was not a utopian. In the meantime historical information had to be provided for the clergy to make them understand the meaning and value of the liturgy.

Still, one area not blocked by finicky rubricism was that of the arts. Regarding music, the restoration of Gregorian Chant, ordered by Pius X and entrusted to the Abbey of Solesmes, aided the goals of the liturgical movement. What better way to help the people participate in the liturgy than by chant? The magazine would naturally have to deal with Gregorian Chant. The same was true for liturgical vestments and church decorations; a battle had to be fought against all the ugliness which had invaded the sanctuary. Enough criticism had been directed toward Saint Sulpice art to make it worthwhile to treat this topic. The magazine had to keep the clergy up to date about the renewal of Christian art. All this took up enough space in the magazine, and it could have been misleading. Some people could see the liturgical movement only as an estheticism designed to make the house of God more attractive and draw crowds to it. But this was not Dom Beauduin's intention, and his personal contribution to the magazine showed it. Renewed esteem for the liturgy was not a question of pastoral tactics but of theological truth. He had begun drafting a manual of basic liturgy, and he published several chapters in the magazine. His reflections were spurred on by a controversy with Père Navatel, the Jesuit editor of the Paris review Études. For this good priest the liturgy was just a code of good manners, a protocol for the Lord's official receptions; but it was something marginal to true piety. Evidently this was a case of the old mix-up between liturgy and rubrics; but beyond this misunderstanding lay two divergent tendencies, each of which was ultimately based on a different theology of the church. A confrere from Maredsous put his finger on the problem by publishing two volumes of stunning erudition entitled, *La liturgie: Essai de synthèse,* and they were more explosive than all the writings of Dom Beauduin.

Dom Maurice Festugière was a Frenchman, a former naval officer. He was a small, thin man and very nervous. I think he did well to give up his career in the navy because, for as much as I knew of him, he lacked practicality, and I doubt that he'd ever have reached the rank of admiral. The story goes that, the first time he served as thurifer, he arrived at the altar holding in one hand an empty censer and in the other a container with burning charcoals hanging from the end of a hook made of wire. He spoke and wrote French with somewhat archaic purity, yet with extreme precision. He was one of the most cultured men I've ever met. Whether it was literature, history, or especially philosophy, he seemed to have read everything. And there was no limit to his willingness to help. When a student of philosophy asked information of him, he'd put himself out to provide it, that is, he'd supply such an exhaustive documentation that the poor fellow would be totally drowned in it. This is also the defect of his *Essai de synthèse:* he was unable to limit himself. This discourages readers, and the work is no longer around today; this is a shame because those two volumes contain treasures of erudition and perceptive insights. We won't sum up this work here, but we should recall one of its conclusions: the Jesuits favored the development of a Catholic religious individualism to compete with Protestantism. I will not pass judgment on the particular responsibility of the Jesuits, but I think Dom Festugière saw things correctly and that the current ill was really a religious individualism which showed up in areas other than the liturgy. The book naturally caused a bit of a stir, but the polemics were on a level beyond that of the average clergyman.

Aside from this episode, the liturgical movement did not appear to be aggressive; but if the liturgy was to regain all its value, one could not avoid shoving a little so as to put certain overly intrusive devotions back in their true place. Lent was eclipsed by the month of Saint Joseph, Paschal Time by the month of Mary. June was dedicated to the Sacred Heart, October to the rosary. Leo XIII had prescribed the recitation of the rosary during Low Masses of that month. Eucharistic piety had evolved toward adoration and exposition of the blessed sacrament. The summit was Mass with exposition of the blessed sacrament. Today this practice has completely disappeared, and no one is complaining. But to criticize it at that time would have scandalized pious persons, especially in those religious institutes founded for the adoration of the blessed sacrament. Priests could skip through the Mass, but they'd be guilty if they didn't make a fifteen minute thanksgiving. One criterion of piety was the recitation of the rosary. A priest who didn't say at least one rosary per day was suspected of lacking all devotion for the Blessed Mother. No matter if he'd recite the *Ave Maria* before each hour of the office and the marian antiphon afterward, it was better to babble through the breviary to have more time to pray afterward. No one would have dreamed of inviting priests to say the hours of the office together during clergy retreats. It was preferable to increase rosaries and stations of the cross. The point was not to criticize these devotions, respectable in themselves, but to reestablish a scale of values which had been distorted. However, by trying to give back to the official prayer of the church its primacy and spiritual value, one inevitably devalued certain devotions, and this didn't please everyone. It brought about some opposition to the liturgical movement, but this was more passive than active, and there wasn't much controversy afterward.

The abbey published some booklets. The main one was *La piété de l'Église* in which Dom Beauduin presented his thoughts about the nature of the liturgy. Another was entitled *La liturgie des défunts,* and a third *Le rituel pour tous.* Perhaps the latter might have raised a question later on for historians of the liturgy. In the wedding Mass you can read a triple "Lamb of God who takes away the sins of the world, grant them rest," with the additional word "eternal" after the third "rest." Since the format for both booklets was the same, the text of the *La liturgie des défunts* was repeated but poorly edited.

Still, most important was the organization of the Liturgical Weeks. These are known through the publication of the *Cours et conférences,* but this series gives only an incomplete idea. First of all, it was Dom Beauduin's desire that the liturgical movement reach both parts of Belgium. The counterpart of *Questions liturgiques et paroissiales* was the Flemish *Liturgisch Tijdschrift* for which he had asked the collaboration of our venerable abbey of Affligem in Brabant. Some liturgical weeks in Flemish were also organized at Mont César. Those in French did not begin in 1912 with that held in Maredsous (whose reports were published in the first volume of *Cours et conférences*): the first occurred in 1910 and it was this, as indicated above, which I attended; the second was held in 1911.

Not very many people took part in these weeks. Participation was reserved to priests and, practically speaking, the forty free rooms in the abbey were enough to house them. Some priests from France were present for the French-speaking weeks, among them Msgr. Harscouët who was rector at the Saint Brieuc Seminary before becoming bishop of Chartres. At the Flemish-speaking weeks there were as many, if not more, Dutch as Flemish participants. You could see some very distinctive people. The most picturesque was Pastor Beukering, a hefty Dutchman, with a jovial face on top of his triple chin. Dom Franco de Wyels, a monk of Affligem, later on would follow Dom Beauduin in his ecumenical undertakings and then return to Affligem where he became abbot. Msgr. Callewaert, a professor at the Bruges Seminary, was the only liturgist in Belgium with true expertise. He had solid scholarly training and was a competent worker. Still, he was a modest man, and a goodly number of his works were laid away in the Bruges diocesan magazine, the *Collationes Brugenses*. His disciple, Dom Eligius Dekkers, did us the favor of collecting Msgr. Callewaert's writings in one volume entitled *Sacris erudiri*.

Please don't ask me what was said in the talks during those weeks. My collaboration in the liturgical movement was completely material, especially consisting in carrying chairs and washing dishes all day long. This was all rather tiring, especially when there were two sessions for sacristans and parish organists in addition to the two others for the priests. But we did it all with good spirits because the atmosphere was excellent. The participants looked satisfied and often enthusiastic.

When I view these facts in hindsight, at a distance of almost sixty years, I am convinced that these first years were decisive. There were no spectacular results nor any grandiose plans. No one had an inkling of the future expansion of the liturgical movement, not only in Catholicism but also in Protestantism, nor that it would have such a deep influence on the life of the church. It would contribute to the progress of the theology of the church and would open onto ecumenism. This was unforeseeable at the time, but the movement started out well and nothing would stop its momentum. It had to set goals and methods. The goal was to get people to participate in the liturgical actions and make communities of prayer out of our assemblies. The method was a return to the sources, the study of tradition. This doesn't mean that it was a movement in reverse. It was turned toward the future, but it had to seek its norms in Scripture and tradition so as not to veer off course. I am sometimes annoyed at hearing talk of liturgy "for twentieth century people." A liturgy is not put together by the century. If this had been done for the people of the nineteenth century according to the then current piety, it would have to be thrown into the wastebasket today. The anaphora of Hippolytus' *Apostolic Tradition* was composed in Rome at the beginning of the third century and was used for more than a thousand years in faraway Ethiopia. It has now been introduced into the *Roman Missal.* This anaphora indeed seems to me to be more worthy of twentieth century people than the rubbish heard today in some churches. The essential thing for a liturgy is not its belonging to one century or to one nation, but the fact that it's Christian, that is, the expression of the faith of the church which belongs to all times.

The liturgical movement had been well launched. It would not stop. But here, for me at least, there was a gap. Another Liturgical Week was announced for the beginning of August 1914 at Mont César, and all was in readiness for the participants. I was supposed to attend it but, when the drama of Sarajevo broke loose, I was busy at Maredsous taking my final exams in philosophy. I didn't have time to finish them. The Belgian government declared a general mobilization and, as a reserve militiaman, I was automatically called to active duty. The police, moreover, were so kind as to remind me of my military obligations. One fine morning I went down to the Denée train station—today it's the storehouse of the abbey's cheese factory—supplied with lunch and a good bottle of wine given me by good Br. Ignatius who had a tear in the corner of his eye. I met Dom Donatien De Bruyne down there as he was on his way to say Mass in a nearby village. Together we boarded the local train from Tamines to Dinant. Dom Donatien was a genuine scholar who had traveled a lot in Germany. He explained to me—stuttering as he always did—that there wouldn't be any war, that it was impossible, that German scholars would get up and protest, all as one man. I didn't attach much importance to the illusions of this scholarly confrere; but I still didn't think that I was going away for five years. I would be discharged only on 15 August, 1919.

4

A New Start

The locale of the action here is still Belgium, though Botte speaks of a growing number of collaborators and the early stirrings of the contemporary liturgical movement in other countries, especially in Germany and neighboring Austria where so many writers were active between the World Wars. Botte takes the opportunity to give a concise evaluation of the Benedictine Odo Casel's theory of the mysteries and its importance for the liturgy. He also offers his own insights as to why Dom Lambert Beauduin left Belgium and his leadership role to teach in Rome. Botte pays tribute to other centers of liturgical activity in the 1920s—mostly monastic centers— including "Saint John's Abbey at Collegeville in America." Some monks from Solesmes Abbey traveled to the United States at this time to lecture on Gregorian Chant. (Tr.)

T HE WAR OF 1914 MARKED A HALT for the workers of the liturgical movement. During my stay at the front I had no direct contact with Mont César, but one day I received a card from Dom Beauduin, postmarked Bournemouth. Through him I learned the details of what had happened in Louvain and especially at the abbey. It had just missed being destroyed, thanks to the scruples and the good sense of a German officer who had awaited a counter-order before carrying out his orders. We tried to find him after the war. Sad to say, he had been killed in Russia, but we showed an interest in his sister, the only living member of his family. As for Dom Beauduin, he became involved in things which had nothing to do with the liturgy and in time was forced to disappear. Nonetheless, he was arrested in the wine cellar of a rectory where he hid himself behind some large butter vats. Led before a military tribunal for interrogation, he was put under armed guard in a separate room of the local town hall. There the soldier started to doze off and then fell asleep. Dom Beauduin realized it was time to tiptoe out of the place; only, there was another guard at the entrance of the town hall. So Dom Beauduin acted with great daring and, relying on the German he knew, said something that was supposed to mean "Thank God I'm free." The guard understood because he smiled sympathetically. Dom Beauduin was condemned to death *in absentia*, but he ended up crossing the Dutch border after other equally fantastic adventures, and he continued working for the British intelligence services. I met him twice during the war while I was on furlough. The first time was at Edermine in Ireland's County Wexford where a few monks of Maredsous had founded a little community. Dom Beauduin rented a nearby house to lodge Belgian soldiers on furlough. He welcomed, among others, some Flemish seminarians. Now at that time a wave of pro-Flemish sentiment was current in the Belgian army. All of a sudden the War Department suspected this house of being a pro-Flemish center, and it forbade any leave permissions for that destination. The second and last time I met Dom Beauduin was in London at the end of August 1918. I can still see us walking at night around Victoria Station where I was going to take the night train for Folkstone. We didn't talk about liturgy. Dom Beauduin must have had other worries. As for myself, I was going to rejoin the sixth chasseur regiment at La Panne where it was being held in reserve for the next offensive. I knew that in a few weeks I would have a front row seat at the fireworks, and this wasn't the time to be making long-term plans.

Dom Beauduin returned to Mont César ahead of me and got back to work. He published the fifth volume of *Questions liturgiques et paroissiales*, dated 1918-1919.

Even though work had been interrupted by the war, the seed sown in the preceding years had germinated in countries other than Belgium. I'm not speaking about Holland which had from the beginning been affected by the Flemish liturgical weeks. The first country where the liturgical movement took root was Italy. From 1914, before the war, the Benedictine abbey of Finalpia began publishing *Revista Liturgica*. But it was Germany which provided the strongest support for the liturgical movement—with somewhat of a delay because of the war and the pitiful situation of the postwar period. All the same, there were no improvisations. In 1921 the *Jahrbuch für Liturgiewissenschaft* came out under the direction of Dom Odo Casel, a monk of the Rheinland abbey of Maria Laach. Then the same monastery established two series: one for publishing liturgical texts, the other for research pieces directed by Dom Cunibert Mohlberg whom I mentioned earlier. Later they were united into one series, *Liturgiegeschichtliche Quellen und Forschungen* (or LQF), in which I published my critical edition of Saint Hippolytus' *Apostolic Tradition* in 1963. Finally, there was a series that aimed at a wider audience and hoped to make the spirit of the liturgy known, namely, *Ecclesia Orans* directed by Dom Ildefonse Herwegen. This publication showed that the other two series were not pure erudition but were intended to help renew the liturgical life of the church. From the beginning Dom Beauduin depended upon the latest works of the French liturgists of the period. Still, it was evident that a more thorough study of tradition would permit a better understanding of the meaning of the rites and texts. Dom Casel, the director of the *Jahrbuch*, set about deepening liturgical theology by his doctrine of mystery theology. His attempt received mixed reviews and is still being debated today. The sometimes violent opposition it encountered derived in part from a misunderstanding.

A number of independent critics have tried to explain Christianity's origins not by doctrinal development but by the influence of the mystery cults. One's first impression might be that Dom Casel seemed to agree with them. Thus this new theology was suspect. But Dom Casel's thought was entirely different. He used as his indisputable starting point the fact that the mystery cults from the Orient had spread throughout the entire Roman Empire. From this it could be deduced that the cults responded to some religious aspirations which were not being satisfied by the cold official rites. Wasn't this, as was true for philosophy, a preparation for Christianity? Consequently once Christianity had arrived, the language of these cults was found to be a means for expressing the mystery of Christ to the Hellenistic world. There's nothing objectionable to faith in this. The issue is to see if the hypothesis is historically justifiable. My thought is that Dom Casel made the error of transforming a hypothesis into a thesis, that he sought proof by forcing the meanings of the texts. For example, it seems impossible to me to explain Saint Paul by the language of the mystery cults. But you can judge the work of Dom Casel from another perspective, namely, that of theology. I have no special competence in this matter because I've never been good at speculation. All the same, I'll allow myself to give my opinion, for what it's worth. The Greek word *mysterion* was translated in Latin as *sacramentum*. All the efforts of Western theology dealt with the meaning of the word, and they reached a theory of the sacraments in which these are distinguished from the other rites by the modality of their effects. The other rites are placed among the *sacramentals*, and the relationship of this category with the sacraments is not easily seen. I do not believe that Christians in the Eastern rites, in the patristic era, reached such a precise solution. I once attended a talk given by a Russian Orthodox who listed the blessing of water among the sacraments. Innocently, I ventured to ask for the Greek word for "sacramental." He didn't know, and none of the Orthodox present could tell me. I concluded that it was a word borrowed from Latin (rite) theology. As a result the term *mysterion* doesn't have the same restricted meaning , and it is open to a wider usage. Dom Casel's use of the term allows for the liturgy a coherent overall vision which does not distinguish rites according to the modalities of their effects but, quite the opposite, brings them together in unity. Thus for baptism you'd distinguish the sacrament (according to the traditional theory, that is, by matter and form) from the secondary rites which are sacramentals; but you can also consider the overall reality which leads to the same objective: participation in the mystery of Christ. The liturgical year is not a sacrament, but it too is a way of participating in the Christian mystery. It seems to me, then, that Dom Casel's theory, independently of its historical foundation, allows us to better understand the liturgy. In any event, during these past years it has allowed Protestants to gain a better understanding of the church's tradition.

One of the good features of the Maria-Laach school was having university professors like Anton Baumstark as collaborators. The forefront of liturgical research was henceforth located in Germany. In the preceding century it was in England, or more exactly, in the Anglican Church.

Another center of the liturgical movement was the abbey of Canons Regular at Klosterneuburg in Austria, through the impetus given by Father Pius Parsch. His aim was essentially pastoral and practical. He pressed for the use of German in some parts of the liturgy. The numerous publications of Pius Parsch had great success in Germany. Other Benedictine monasteries were also centers of liturgical activity, such as the Portugese monastery of Singeverga where Dom Antonio Coehlo (whom I mentioned earlier) founded the review *Opus Dei* in 1926, and at Saint John's Abbey at Collegeville in America.

In France there was no organized movement before World War II. In this regard France depended on Belgium. Still, there was one thing that gave particular joy to Dom Beauduin. It was the conversion, if we could put it this way, of the magazine *Études*. The editor of the magazine, Father Navatel, was the first and the most combative of Dom Beauduin's opponents. Then, all of a sudden, a new editor declared himself to be an enthusiastic advocate of the liturgical movement, and he was no unknown. Père Paul Doncoeur had written a sensational article in *L'homme libre*, Gustave Hervé's journal. The religious who had been expelled from France returned to serve in the French army (during World War I), but in peacetime the French laws remained in effect and there was talk of enforcing the law which had sent the religious into exile. That was when Père Doncoeur wrote his article "We Will Not Leave" ("Nous ne partirons pas"). Published in a leftist journal, the article was a sensation and helped make the government act prudently. Père Doncoeur's praise of the liturgical movement was not a simple act of politeness made in passing; it was an expression of profound conviction. I knew him twenty-five years later: he was still as enthusiastic as ever and remained so till the end of his life.

Earlier on I mentioned that France remained under the influence of Belgium. It should be noted that a new center for the liturgical apostolate was created in Belgium at the Abbey of Saint-André through the impetus given by Dom Gaspard Lefebvre.

Dom Lefebvre was from the North of France, and he had entered the Abbey of Maredsous. From there he followed Dom Gerard van Caloen who was entrusted with reforming the Benedictine Congregation of Brazil which had fallen into complete decline. To find young men ready to repopulate the empty monasteries, they established a recruitment center near Bruges. This small foundation was the nucleus of the Abbey of Saint-André, established in 1912. It shifted direction by accepting a mission in Katanga. Dom Lefebvre returned from Brazil and became a member of the Saint-André community. During World War I the abbey was occupied by the Germans, and the monks were scattered. Dom Lefebvre took advantage of this forced leisure time to prepare a *Daily Missal* which is well known. What people generally do not know is that he followed the steps of Dom Gerard van Caloen, the reformer of the Brazilian Congregation. The only Latin-French missal existing at that time was produced by Desclée-Tournai: its editor was Dom van Caloen. This book was incomplete, unhandy, and not very widely used. Dom Lefebvre's missal, on the other hand, had long-lasting success and was translated into many languages. It contained not only the text and translation of the liturgical prayers, but also commentaries and appendices for the sacraments. Dom Lefebvre also composed a little missal adapted for children, then a weekly *Bulletin* specifically designed for sacristans and teaching sisters, and finally school materials with teachers' outlines.

Dom Lefebvre was a tireless worker and had organizational sense. He was criticized for working with scissors and glue. I think this is true because some of the fascicles of the *Dictionnaire d'archéologie chrétienne et de liturgie* were found with pages cut apart at those passages which corresponded to articles of Dom Lefebvre in his *Bulletin*. But Dom Cabrol, the learned author of the *Dictionnaire* used to do just about the same thing, and this was a fair repayment. Furthermore, Dom Lefebvre never laid claim to originality. He aimed at providing information for just a small public. The *Bulletin paroissial et liturgique* answered questions raised by its readers. Sometimes these were naive, and this once led a confrere to come up with a hoax. The editor received a letter written in France by the superior of the Purification Sisters. The point of the inquiry was that these sisters had inherited from their founder a chasuble of woven silk in two colors, red and green, so that—according to changes in lighting—the chasuble showed up as green or red. What were they to do? Stand all the servers on the same side, or cover the windows on one side so that the people would see only the prescribed color? The *Bulletin* published the letter and tried to solve this distressing problem—perhaps evidence of naiveté, but also a sign of courtesy toward the readership. Whatever the gaps in Dom Lefebvre's work, we must acknowledge that it was of key importance in France. The missal could be found in everyone's hand from childhood on, and it wasn't only a prayerbook but also a tool for teaching religion. The *Bulletin* answered the needs of a public which didn't receive replies from the more learned review which has become its successor, namely, *Paroisse et liturgie.*

Questions liturgiques et paroissiales began publication right after the war, as I said; but it was not till 1924 that the Liturgical Weeks recommenced. Dom Beauduin spoke at the first one, but the printed report attached a new title to his name, that of liturgy professor at Saint Anselm's College in Rome. He had left Mont César at the beginning of the 1923-1924 school year. Why did he leave the abbey and, for all purposes, the liturgical movement? Did he already have his sights set upon the ecumenical apostolate? I don't believe so. The reasons for his leaving are simple, but also more ticklish to explain. When we returned from the war the community had grown considerably. There were about ten faces I didn't recognize. Among them was Dom Odo Lottin, a former university professor who was well known for his works on medieval theology. He had entered the monastery a few days before the war. After his novitiate he became professor of theology and prefect of studies. He was an influential individual in the community. Although not hostile to the liturgical movement, he wasn't enthusiastic about it. What he heard from those who attended the prewar Liturgical Weeks left an impression on him. Four weeks' study out of two months' vacation was perhaps a little too much. He was afraid of the exuberant activity of Dom Beauduin and told him so. I didn't learn this from Dom Beauduin, but from Dom Lottin himself. On the other hand, the young men who had entered the monastery during the war, except for Dom Maurus Grégoire of whom I'll speak later on, didn't know Dom Beauduin, and none of them seemed interested in the liturgical movement. I myself had to make up the years lost during the war. Dom Beauduin felt a little isolated. The abbot of Montserrat had written asking him to receive two monks of his abbey to train them in liturgy. As he told me this, Dom Beauduin began to laugh and added: "What am I supposed to do? I'm all alone here." He surely felt somewhat confined and thought he'd be of more use at an international school than at Mont César. Did he take the initiative or did this come from the Abbot Primate in Rome? I don't know. When I was at Saint Anselm's College from 1919-1920 there was no liturgy course, just two or three conferences given by Dom Ildefonsus Schuster, then abbot of Saint Paul-Outside-the-Walls and later on archbishop of Milan. The Abbot Primate probably felt the need for a real liturgy course. Dom Joseph Kreps, whom I have already briefly mentioned, took over the magazine.

Dom Kreps was from Antwerp. After a year of philosophy at the Malines minor seminary he entered Mont César. He had an aptitude for music, but he admitted that he knew nothing about it at that time. When he entered, the organist was Dom Ermine Vitry who founded the children's choir, but Dom Vitry returned to Maredsous, and Dom Joseph took his place and retained it till his death. He improved his musical education by taking courses at the Lemmens Institute in Malines, but he worked especially by himself and acquired absolute proficiency. He not only possessed good technique, but he was a real artist—including the good qualities and defects which that involves. He was completely unconventional, indifferent to whatever was certain to happen. He used to show up in the community with a four-day-old beard, and this led to a joke on the part of a confrere. By custom a bouquet of flowers appeared on the refectory table in front of the place of the monk whose nameday it was. Well, on the feast of Saint Joseph Dom Kreps found at his place a magnificent cactus. He laughed kind-heartedly at it. He carried out the job of organist with enthusiasm, but with the realization that his art was at the service of the liturgy. During a stay at Solesmes he was invited to accompany the conventual Mass. At recreation one of the priests asked the cantor what he thought of the accompaniment. The latter simply replied that he hadn't noticed anything and that he didn't know who had played the organ. Dom Kreps said that this was the nicest compliment he had received. At a congress he once expounded his theory on the unifying role of the organist: the organist was supposed to link the various chant pieces together while keeping the same tonality. Never did he introduce an unfamiliar selection into the office. Instead, his improvisations were always on themes from the chants.

Till his death Dom Kreps also maintained the same zeal while directing the children's choir. He had his own way of running his little world. When howling was heard, no one would get upset: we knew it was Dom Joseph directing a rehearsal. Yet the children liked him a lot, and they long remembered their time in the choir. Two years ago I met a former choir-member leaving church, who today has become an important lawyer at the Assize Court in Brussels. He told me: "Do you know why I came here today? It's the fiftieth anniversary of my joining the choir."

Dom Kreps' musical knowledge was vast. He was very well acquainted with the history of the organ, and he collaborated with an important organ builder in Bonn. But he was particularly interested in musical paleography and medieval musicology. He did not agree with the theories of the Solesmes school concerning the interpretation of the rhythmical signs. It is unfortunate that nothing positive was produced by all the time he devoted to this research. He was intelligent and had some correct insights, but he lacked method and often got lost on the tangents he encountered. At one point I tried to work with him, but I had to give it up.

It was Dom Kreps who was in charge of the magazine and the Liturgical Weeks. The latter recommenced in 1924 but with a different rhythm. One year they were held at Mont César; the following year in another city. When this occurred, they were directed not only toward the clergy but also the laity, and liturgies were organized in different parishes. The first session after the war was held at Malines. It was only in 1927 that I spoke for the first time, giving a paper on the invocation of Christ in the Foremass. Held at Mont César, this session had as its presider Dom Bernard Capelle, a monk of Maredsous.

It would be unfair not to mention Dom Maurus Grégoire among the new collaborators. He was one of the earliest supporters. As Père Alphonse Grégoire he addressed the 1911 Liturgical Week at Maredsous, at a time when he was professor of liturgy at the Tournai seminary. He entered Mont César during the war. He was an intelligent, spiritual man, and easy to get along with. He submitted several articles to the magazine. Unfortunately, he had a tortuous mind. He had been appointed professor of liturgy and, as is proper, began his course with a definition of liturgy. With imprudence he opened a parenthesis before completing his definition, and the parenthesis was never closed. He provided, as a supplement to the magazine, models of liturgical homilies.

Although Msgr. Camille Callewaert was the most competent among the professors in Belgium's seminaries, Canon August Croegaert, professor at Malines, was the most dynamic. Tall and serious looking, he had a childlike face and certain mannerisms which made him look a bit ridiculous. His classes were bedlam.

Much later, a pastor from Brussels, reminiscing about his younger days, started mimicking him. Then he added: "Well, then, it's the only course which was actually helpful in my ministry. He gave a theological synthesis, and he was so deeply convinced that you couldn't help being impressed."

During the years immediately following the war the liturgical movement became both widespread and reinforced. It became more popular and saw some immediate results. It benefited from favorable circumstances, especially from the development of Catholic Action, in particular the Young Christian Workers movement. Father Cardijn was a friend of the abbey, and from the start of his apostolate he used to come for periods of recollection with his first members. When he began to organize large meetings, he entrusted the task of preparing the Mass to the abbey since the Mass was supposed to be the center of the day. Dom Kreps was in charge of rehearsing and directing the chant. He did so with his usual zest and became a familiar face in the YCW movement. To be sure, these meetings of young workers, with responses made to the priest, with singing the ordinary parts of the Mass, with participation in the offertory and communion, helped the liturgical movement gain more ground than many articles.

There was also an evolution in piety at this time. Among the spiritual writers who showed a return toward a biblically inspired doctrinal piety was Dom Columba Marmion, the abbot of Maredsous. What was his influence on the liturgical movement? This question was asked by an irascible Dominican in 1948. According to him, Dom Marmion didn't understand much about the liturgical movement and even allowed one of his monks to publish in a Brussels newspaper a veritable tract against the movement. I understand the irritation of this Dominican in regard to the posthumous edition of the last writings of Dom Marmion, but this is no reason to behave unfairly. It's true that in 1912 an anonymous article against the liturgical movement appeared. It seems likely that this article was the work of a monk of Maredsous. Canonically, a superior is responsible for what one of his subjects writes, on condition that he had given his permission. If the Dominican priest had known the assumed author as I knew him, he would have acted more prudently. I am quite sure he didn't request anything of anybody. He was an old eccentric who just followed his own fancy. He was in charge of welcoming pilgrims and maintaining order in the church. Well, one Sunday he noticed an elegant

lady seated in the pews reserved for the men, next to a young ec-
clesiastic who could be taken for a Frenchman because he wasn't
wearing a Roman collar like Belgian priests. Reverend-Father-
Policeman pounced on the lady and, with an imperious gesture,
sent her to the women's side of the church with these words: "Go,
Madame, instead of billing and cooing with your little French
abbé." The lady was the Baroness de Gaiffier d'Estroy, wife of the
governor of the Namur Province, and the little French abbé was
her son, today a well-known Bollandist. This learned Jesuit will
not hold it against me for revealing this episode from his youth
which contains nothing derogatory either with regard to his
mother or to him. The abbot of Maredsous was not responsible for
this outburst, no more than he was for many others. Nor is there
any reason to believe that he was responsible for the offending article; in fact, Dom Marmion proved himself favorable to the movement. He had approved the work of Dom Festugière and had just
welcomed to his monastery the Liturgical Week of 1911. It is possible that he did not always grasp all the facets of the liturgical
movement, but this is not what is in question. Did his writings,
willy-nilly, have an influence on liturgical life? As far as I'm concerned, I think so. I attended his Sunday conferences during the
year 1913-1914 up to the general mobilization. He spoke at
length, without any notes. He gave points of an outline but rarely
did he cover all of it. I have the best recollections of these conferences, and I don't believe I was ever bored, something which
doesn't apply to many others. You'd wish that many preachers
were as familiar with Saint Paul as he was and took their inspiration from him in their preaching.

Does Dom Marmion deserve to be canonized? This is a question that does not come under my competence, but I must admit
that I'd never have dreamed of it on my own. I had much respect
for him, and he was friendly toward me. He told inane stories, like
the one about the Englishman who had a fine pair of shoes and
who ordered the hotel bellhop not to rub them with a brush but to
"polissonner avec une lingère," that is, "to act naughty with the
linen maid." This gave no offense to my ears, which never were
particularly delicate. I also know that he wouldn't turn down a
shot of wiskey. In 1915 I took a furlough in Ireland. I arrived at
Edermine on the morning of the day Dom Marmion was supposed to leave. Since there weren't many rooms, the guestmaster
awaited Dom Marmion's departure to put me in his room. We

found there a flask of whiskey, already mostly gone, because I emptied what was left with one swig. I don't know if this would be an obstacle to canonization. Since I was not called in to testify, no question of conscience was raised for me. Personally I have no reason to complain. Dom Marmion had the charity to leave me the taste of a good glass, while he could have emptied the flask before leaving. Anyway, this adds no weight to a judgment on the influence of Dom Marmion's writings. I am convinced that it was deep and beneficial to the liturgical movement.

5

Dom Bernard Capelle

Dom Bernard Capelle, another transfer to the Benedictines from the diocesan clergy (as was Dom Beauduin) brought scholarly knowledge of the Bible to his role in the liturgical movement. He enlarged the target audience for the liturgy courses he taught at Mont César by inviting religious and diocesan seminarians studying elsewhere in Louvain to attend. Botte reveals the sobering truth that neither he nor Dom Capelle ever took any liturgy courses during their studies for the priesthood. Botte mentions the universal priesthood of the faithful, a major concern of his for almost a quarter-century. (Tr.)

T HE FIRST LITURGICAL WEEK I ATTENDED as a speaker was held in August 1927. Its theme was the first part of the Mass, and it was presided over by a monk of Maredsous, Dom Bernard Capelle, who was then very little known. The following March he was elected coadjutor-abbot of Mont César, and thereafter he would occupy an important place in the liturgical movement.

Paul Capelle came from Namur. After his studies in humanities at Our Lady of Peace secondary school run by the Jesuits of that same city, he joined the diocesan clergy; but instead of following the usual progression from minor to major seminary, he was sent to the Belgian College in Rome where he stayed for eleven years.

After obtaining doctorates in philosophy and theology at the Gregorianum he continued his training by earning a doctorate in biblical studies with a thesis on the African Psalter.

After such long and specialized training one would have thought he'd be made professor of Sacred Scripture at the Namur major seminary, all the more so considering the notorious deficiencies of the then current professor. Nothing of the sort happened. The good canon stayed on for another fifteen years. As for Abbé Capelle, he was sent to be assistant pastor in the little city of Gembloux. He performed his ministry for a few years and then, toward the end of the war, he entered the abbey of Maredsous where he received the name of Bernard. What caused this change of direction? I really don't know. Certainly it was not spite over not being made a seminary professor. If he was looking for honors, he would not have shut himself up in a monastery. I think that experience had shown him that he wasn't cut out for parish ministry. One day he made a mistake he could not forget since I heard him tell the story more than once. A woman of Gembloux had just lost her son. To console her, Abbé Capelle told her that God chastens those he loves. The woman rebelled on the spot and stopped practicing religion entirely. Years later, when he was abbot of Mont César, Dom Capelle still went to Gembloux to visit this lady. I never found out whether he was able to bring her to a more positive attitude. He certainly lacked psychological insight and did not always understand those speaking to him. Be that as it may, he entered Maredsous and was perfectly happy there.

After his profession he was appointed editor of the *Revue bénédictine,* a task for which his studies prepared him well. His thesis on the African Psalter made him familiar with Tertullian, Cyprian, and Augustine. This was entirely in line with the tradition of the *Revue bénédictine.* Dom Capelle enhanced interest in the publication by adding to it the supplement, the *Bulletin d'ancienne littérature latine chrétienne.* This bulletin reviewed everything being published on the ancient Latin versions of the Bible and on the Latin Fathers. Everything was going along fine when happenstance changed the flow of things. After the war Maredsous and Mont César separated themselves from the Congregation of Beuron and united themselves to the abbey of Saint-André which had left the Brazilian Congregation. Thus the Belgian Congregation was founded. The general chapter decided that theological studies would be done at Mont César. Now, one year there was one less theology professor. Dom Capelle was called in and, as a result, he spent a year at Mont César. He was an excellent professor of theology but, beyond that, he also won the friendship of the community. This was why he was invited to preside at the 1927 Liturgical Week. The next year the community had to face a problem. The founding abbot, Dom Robert de Kerchove, was getting old and was no longer up to his job. He resigned, and the chapter had to choose a coadjutor with the right of succession. Dom Capelle was unanimously elected. I've never seen a more clear-cut election, and had it not been for the formalities of canon law, it would have gone more quickly, for we were all in agreement before we started the meeting. For someone seeking honors it would have been a triumph; for Dom Capelle it was a disaster. He was so deeply attached to the monastery of his profession, to his confreres, to his work, that to leave them was a painful separation for him. The monk in the cell next to his heard him crying, but it was a question of conscience for Dom Capelle. Could he, to assure his own personal tranquility, reject the unanimous call the community was sending him? He accepted, but for a long time he was filled with nostalgia for Maredsous, and I'm not sure it ever disappeared entirely.

His mission was delicate. He became coadjutor to an old abbot who was retaining his title, but without real jurisdiction. This was a hybrid canonical solution which had disastrous effects in other abbeys. But in the case of Mont César it did not go wrong, especially thanks to the admirable honesty of the old abbot who refrained from any further interventions. Perhaps he was not always content, but he never showed it. Dom Capelle had the greatest reverence for him and made efforts to treat him tactfully.

Dom Capelle was then at full strength: not very tall but robust, sturdily built, a little on the stout side. One day I gave him quite a scare. During recreation we went to the farm and came up with the idea of weighing ourselves. Dom Capelle got on the large pan of the scale while a confrere put weights on the small pan. At 176 pounds (80 kilos) Dom Capelle showed a bit of uneasiness, but the scale didn't budge. At 187 and then at 198 pounds his worry grew; but at 209 pounds he looked so upset that I removed my foot from the pan of the scale. In spite of his stoutness and his reputation for slowness which, rightly or wrongly, is ascribed to natives of Namur, he was alert and remained so till the end. His walk was brisk, his gestures brusque and nervous. Habitually he cut open the pages of books and magazines with a sharp letter opener and regularly left holes in the inside margins. Being librarian, I ventured to offer him a boxwood paper cutter with a rounded point. In the refectory he gobbled down his meal with a speed that visibly irritated old Abbot Robert who told him: "I admire you a lot. You seem to have no taste for food, you stuff it into yourself as if it were hay." Dom Capelle protested that he did not dislike earthly foods and excused himself by saying it was a holdover from his years of ministry when he took his meals in haste between one activity and the other. He didn't change his ways and continued to "put away the hay."

Dom Capelle was cheerful and jovial, full of kindness in his relations with others. But, as I said, he sometimes lacked insight and didn't always find the proper gesture or word. He was a poor diplomat, and I reproached him more than once for letting himself be taken in; he lacked daring and too easily gave in to the other abbots. The good qualities of Dom Capelle greatly made up for his faults. He accepted his responsibility out of pure dedication, and did not spare any efforts.

At the time he started his job we had decided to publish *Recherches de théologie ancienne et médiévale*. Dom Capelle took his place on the team, but there was also the liturgical movement and the *Questions liturgiques et paroissiales*. He decided to make his own personal contribution to them.

Dom Capelle never took a course in liturgy. He never attended a seminary, and at that time there was no liturgy course at the Gregorian University. But his name appeared among the first subscribers to *Questions liturgiques et paroissiales* at the time he was assistant pastor in Gembloux. On the other hand, his biblical and patristic training and his experience with literary and textual criticism prepared him for studying the liturgy from a new viewpoint. Still, in spite of the scholarly character of his work, he never lost sight of an ultimately pastoral goal, and he did not look down on popularization.

In August 1928 he participated in the Liturgical Week at Tournai which, as always, was organized by Dom Kreps. The topic of the session was the canon of the Mass. I gave a paper on the angel of sacrifice mentioned in the prayer *Supplices te rogamus*. Among the other speakers was Joseph Coppens, at that time a young professor at the School of Theology in Louvain. His paper on the links between the pagan mysteries and the Christian mysteries appeared to me to be a good treatment of the problem. But, and I don't know why, it received a rather cool welcome by Msgr. Battifol who was presiding at the session.

Another speaker I recall is Père Lemonnyer, a Dominican. At the time of the expulsion of the religious, the French Dominicans took refuge at the Saulchoir, near Tournai. Their students were given permission to attend the conferences of the Liturgical Week. Did this influence the Dominicans who organized the liturgical movement in France after the war of 1940? I don't know, but later on I did meet some Dominicans who had heard me speak in 1928.

But let's return to Père Lemonnyer, who was a professor at the Saulchoir. He appropriately gave communion with hosts consecrated at the same Mass. He was an excellent theologian straddling, as it were, two subjects. He was both a biblical scholar and a commentator on Saint Thomas Aquinas. Later on the abbot asked him to preach the community retreat, hoping he would speak about Paul whom he knew so well; but he gave us a commentary on the articles of the *Summa* of Saint Thomas on the virtue of religion, including the article on oaths. He died in Rome, with Père Garrigou-Lagrange at his bedside. Since the latter, true to his origins, southern France, was multiplying invocations and exhortations, Père Lemonnyer told him: "Let me die in peace."

The next year Dom Capelle undertook a new initiative: public courses in liturgy would be given at Mont César, both for our theology students and for religious of other orders, and eventually for students at the School of Theology, since there was no liturgy course at the university at that time. There had been one, a little before the war. It was entrusted to Msgr. Camille Callewaert, but his appointment was not renewed. Since that time there was nothing. The courses Dom Capelle wanted to organize would be held on Tuesday afternoon, from November to Easter, and would last two hours per week. He wanted to have a second professor share these courses with him, and so he asked me to take charge of the second hour. This is how I became a professor of liturgy.

No different from Dom Capelle, I had not taken any liturgy courses. I had spoken twice at the 1918 and 1928 Liturgical Weeks, and I had written a few book reviews for *Questions liturgiques et parossiales*, but this wasn't my trade. After the war it became evident that the way of recruiting theology professors wasn't very well organized. The apparent principle was that anyone could teach anything at all with the blessing of the abbot. Spiritually this was very profitable to those who were appointed because it allowed them to put into practice the chapter in Saint Benedict's *Rule* about the impossible things that could be imposed on a monk. Furthermore, it was said that the best way to learn something was to teach it, and perhaps that's true; but you have to add that it's generally to the detriment of the students. I was the first person sent to the university to get ready for teaching. I was also free to choose my field of work, and I chose Sacred Scripture. Wanting to specialize in textual criticism of the New Testament, I undertook the study of Oriental languages because familiarity with the ancient versions is indispensable for this subject. After finishing my studies I became professor of Sacred Scripture as well as librarian and second cantor. Thus I didn't have any particular training for teaching liturgy. Like Dom Capelle, I was a biblical scholar who wandered into liturgy. I had, however, a good biblical education, and I was also trained in the methods of textual and literary criticism. Besides, my knowledge of Oriental languages opened for me the door to liturgies often poorly known by Western liturgists. Things always work out in my life, even if they go otherwise than expected. If I had been trained to teach liturgy, it's more than likely that I would never have studied Oriental languages. I studied them to do textual criticism of the New Testament, and here life's fortunes presented me with a new direction which turned me away from my goal. I retained from my old trade only the articles on biblical texts and manuscripts of the *Supplément au Dictionnaire de la Bible*.

I also took advantage of my experience as librarian. It's incredible what you learn when you're librarian and you do an honest job of it. I saw a lot of fine people come by who were preparing theses and didn't know where to start. In general, they didn't know the most basic study tools. You had to put these into their hands, if not use them for them. That takes time, but it's part of the job, and you learn a lot. This was the way I learned to sort out the history of the sacramentaries.

The Tuesday liturgy classes were well received. We had a goodly number of students from religious orders, the most numerous being the Jesuits. The first year we spoke about the origins of the Mass. I was in charge of the biblical part, whereas Dom Capelle studied the first patristic and liturgical documents. The next year Dom Capelle studied the paschal cycle and I took the Christmas cycle. This is the course which appeared in revised form under the title *Les origines de la Noël et de l'Epiphanie.*

Dom Capelle was an excellent professor. Not only were his classes well organized, but his delivery was clear and vibrant. His research would lead to a history of the Roman Mass. I suggested adding as an appendix to his book a critical edition of the Roman canon. But since his volume was delayed, I asked to publish separately my edition of the canon and add parallel texts with notes to it.

Those Tuesday classes lasted till World War II, and they began again after the war.

One unexpected result of these classes was Dom Capelle's appointment as a lecturer in liturgy at the university. It would have been simpler to allow the few students involved to take classes at our place, but the university was jealous and would not allow anything to take place right next to it. A liturgy course had to be created in the School of Theology. But there was no worthwhile candidate to teach it, and it would have been ridiculous to appoint some obscure tenure-holder while Dom Capelle was teaching in the same city. So Dom Capelle was appointed—to a phantom course which had no students at all. I'll return to this later on.

The Liturgical Weeks continued to alternate between Louvain and other cities. I don't have special recollections of any of them except for the one which—taking the participation of the faithful in the liturgy as its theme—dealt with the priesthood of the faithful.

This theme was a constant refrain of Catholic Action. A Belgian Jesuit, Père Dabin, had written a large book, *Le sacerdoce royal.* Msgr. Cerfaux wrote a ferocious review of it, one which might have shortened the author's life. A whole complicated system of distinctions was put together: general and special priesthood, ministerial priesthood, active and passive priesthood. What could that have meant? Saint Thomas spoke of a passive participation in the priesthood which meant that you received the effects of the priesthood, something entirely different. Canon Lebon urged Dom Capelle to study the problem in the light of tradition.

Canon Lebon was patristics professor at the School of Theology. He was perfectly competent in the field of the theological and christological controversies of the fourth to sixth centuries, but this intelligent man wore blinders and could never understand how liturgical texts could provide any interest at all for theology.

He had deep contempt for the courses we gave at Mont César, and he dissuaded the few students who showed a desire from taking them. The importance that some liturgists accorded the priesthood of the faithful seemed suspect to him. He was used to doing a meticulous analysis of texts. Well, in the patristic literature he was familiar with he had never come across any expositions on the priesthood of the faithful. It was sort of a challenge which he had thrown at Dom Capelle. The challenge was accepted, and Dom Capelle decided that the topic would be considered at the next Liturgical Week. He called me in and asked me to study the question in the Fathers of the church. I replied that I had no ideas on the subject, and I didn't want to defend a pre-established thesis. I knew liturgists would like to find support in tradition for their theories, but I wasn't sure that my conclusions would correspond to theirs. Dom Capelle replied that what was needed was an impartial inquiry.

Setting to work conscientiously, I examined all the patristic evidence in context. Thus I established a rich dossier. The conclusions that could be drawn from these texts were inescapable. Most of the time there was a purely metaphorical sense without any link to the eucharist. However, there were some texts which linked the priesthood with the post-baptismal anointing, but—in this case—priesthood was never alone: it was placed between kingship and prophethood, following the Old Testament tradition by which anointing is given to the king, the priest, and the prophet. This was evidently only an analogy. The image of the priest evoked the idea of consecration. Besides, to isolate priesthood from kingship and prophethood would distort the meaning. I knew in advance that these conclusions would disillusion my audience, but I was not hired to please them. It was impossible to present all my data in one hour's time. I summarized it, and the outcome was as expected. Dom Lefebvre was disappointed and asked me if more couldn't be found. I wasn't able to guarantee for him that my search was exhaustive, but I replied that not much would change since tradition is not hidden away in some isolated texts but in the overall agreement of witnesses. Msgr. Picard, the chaplain general of Catholic Action, became angry. He declared that this wasn't what was needed but instead something that would fill young people with enthusiasm; that the pope had spoken about the priesthood of the faithful, and that we could continue to do so. I answered him by saying that I wouldn't at all dream of stopping him from speaking about the priesthood of the faithful. I was only asking that he not claim to speak for tradition without having taken the trouble to study it. Canon Lebon was present, and I feel sure that he was the only person satisfied, but I never once thought of the idea of pleasing him.

This happened in 1933. Twenty years later, while visiting Paris, I was invited to a meeting of the editorial board of *La Maison-Dieu*. They were considering doing an issue on the priesthood of the faithful. Since my opinion was asked, I gave it in all simplicity and felt like a heretic uttering blasphemies among the orthodox Fathers. Some texts were cited with which I was well acquainted. I remarked that these could not be interpreted out of their context. All one had to do was read further to notice that it never was a question of the eucharistic offering. Basing the whole liturgical movement on an at least doubtful interpretation of a scriptural text, without any serious foundation in tradition, seemed to me a regrettable error. At Rome there had been some reactions against the abusive way certain theologians used Saint Peter's text on the royal priesthood. The editors of *La Maison-Dieu* wanted to defend an interpretation they considered traditional, but no one had given any serious study to the problem. I mentioned that their approach wasn't very reasonable. That of Dom Capelle's twenty years previously had been much more sound: there was a problem and it had to be studied seriously before taking a position on it. This time, the battle was joined before they even knew the state of the question. No one had read either the outstanding article of Canon Cerfaux on the exegesis of Saint Peter's text nor the paper I gave at Louvain. The first to rally to my position was Canon Mansencaux, from the diocese of Bordeaux if my memory is correct. He remarked that oversimplifications in teaching usually end up with questionable formulations like the one he noticed in the catechism lesson of a good sister: "Baptism makes us children of God and priests of Jesus Christ." In the end, the editors of *La Maison-Dieu* gave up planning an issue on the priesthood of the faithful.

I've jumped ahead twenty years. Let's move back.

6

New Collaborators

Various experts rallied to the liturgical movement in the period between the World Wars: Placide Bruylants (Roman Rite prayer forms), John-Michael Hanssens (Eastern Rites), Odilo Heiming (history of the liturgy), R. J. Hesbert (musical paleography) on the Continent and Gregory Dix (origins of the eucharistic prayer) in England—all receive appreciative treatment in this chapter. Botte alludes to the "considerable" influence on liturgical reform of Joseph Jungmann, the Jesuit theologian and historian whose great showcase work, *The Mass of the Roman Rite*, gave thousands of readers access to the riches of liturgical tradition.

In a pithy sentence Botte sums up Rome's attitude toward the movement at this time: "The reform started by Pius X wasn't buried, only shelved." But the scholarly efforts of these new workers, joined to an awareness of pastoral needs, would pave the way for Vatican II's churchwide call to liturgical renewal. (Tr.)

I T WAS IMPORTANT FOR THE LITURGICAL MOVEMENT to be sustained by research that would keep it in line with tradition. But in order to remain a movement it also had to find expression in concrete achievements among the Christian people. Mont César had a team which organized liturgical days in parishes. Their aim was to help parish priests promote the active participation of the faithful in parishes by instruction, by practicing chant, and by directing the celebrations. The team included

Dom Kreps and Dom Augustin François (former chaplain to the students at the university). They were joined by Dom Pierre Symons who was in charge of the liturgical office for several years. Theirs was low-profile work which has left no trace in history. Still, it was necessary so that the liturgical movement could keep in contact with pastoral realities.

Questions liturgiques et paroissiales was entrusted to Dom Anselm Robeyns who had attended with me the 1933 Liturgical Week on the priesthood of the faithful. In 1972 he reached reached retirement age from his position as liturgy professor at the university's Institute of Religious Studies.

Our greatest collaborator, one whom we had the misfortune to lose in the prime of his life, was Dom Placide Bruylants. The earliest picture I have of him is that of a small fellow with round and red cheeks, dressed in a choir monk's robes and seated prim and proper on his choir bench. He had a beautiful voice, and after a few years had become choirmaster. He did his studies in humanities at Saint Peter's secondary school in Louvain and then entered the novitiate at the abbey. He came from a modest background. His father was a blacksmith. His mother was blind, but this did not hinder her from doing the housework by herself. Dom Bruylants did not hide the fact that his childhood was spent in a certain degree of poverty, although not in indigence, and that he hadn't always eaten to his fill. Being the son of a common laborer caused him no embarrassment—he was more inclined to be proud of it. He was my student for four years, although not a brilliant one as he himself realized. A healthy self-image allowed him to recognize his limitations and possibilities. He knew that with dogged effort he would produce useful work which would suit his ability. And that's exactly what happened.

The first project I proposed to him was the *Concordance du Sacramentaire léonien*. This concordance has a curious history. There was a young girl, a student of mine at the Saint Louis Institute of Religious Studies in Brussels who had a licentiate in business and who was employed by the Banque de Bruxelles. She was bored stiff and became neurasthenic as a result. She was tired of counting numbers all day long and asked me if I could suggest some more useful and intelligent job to take her mind off all the digits. I had already thought that a concordance of the *Leonine (Veronense) Sacramentary* would be a great service, but I didn't have anyone to do the file cards. So, I proposed that this young lady put the sacramentary onto file cards. She was very intelligent. I gave her some lessons in Latin on the side and checked her work from time to time. You might think I have some peculiar methods for healing neurasthenics. A method is judged by its fruits, and in this case the results were excellent from all points of view. The lady was cured. She married, had four children, and today is a grandmother twice over. As for myself, I had about forty thousand cards to be classified. I proposed this task to Dom Placide, and he gladly accepted. Printing the text still had to be done. I never was under the illusion that a publisher would ever agree to publish such a large volume at his own expense, and I didn't have a penny. I thought it would be enough to have the text typed and—to reduce costs—make a few extra carbon copies. So I wrote to some people who'd be interested, in particular Paul Faider. He was professor at the University of Ghent and had been appointed curator at the Mariemont Museum after Flemish became the official language of the university. He was concurrently secretary of the International Union for publishing the new Du Cange Dictionary and director of the *Archivum latinitatis medii aevi (Bulletin du Cange)*. I asked him then to take one copy of the concordance. At the following meeting of the international committee he passed along my offer. Professor Arnaldi, the Italian delegate, reacted as soon as he realized that a manuscript from Verona was involved, and he declared that this pertained exclusively to his country. This was all the more stupid since Arnaldi knew nothing about sacramentaries. He had edited a *Lexicon latinitatis imperfectum,* and not a single sacramentary appeared in his sources. Regardless, there was no more hope in that direction. All the same, a little later on Paul Faider died, and his wife carried on his duties. That was during the war. Paper was requisitioned by the Germans, but the *Bulletin du Cange* had a privileged situation as an international institution. Mrs. Faider had quite a stock of publisher's paper available, but she had no copy and didn't want the paper to go to the Germans. She remembered my correspondence with her husband and wrote me. I sent her a few small articles, but this wasn't enough. I then offered to edit the concordance, and she accepted. I went with Dom Placide to visit her at Mariemont, and all the steps were taken to have the printing done. In this way the International Union didn't provide me with only one typed copy as I had proposed, but had the concordance printed at its own expense in spite of Arnaldi's protestations. By paying only for the paper we were able to have 250 copies made.

There's no doubt that the increase of studies on the *Leonine Sacramentary* was greatly due to this indispensible study tool provided by Dom Bruylants.

This encouraged Dom Bruylants to follow the same path by creating other study tools. Thus he put together a catalogue of *incipit's* and *desinit's* of the sacramentaries, a work which still exists on file cards in the abbey's Documentation Center.

Dom Bruylants knew how to use all well-disposed people. As a result Dom Benoît, who had no intellectual gifts, typed out these cards. To arrange them in order Dom Bruylants called upon a friend whose name was Vital—I never learned his family name—who was a night watchman for a local railroad company. This good fellow spent the night in an office where he had nothing else to do except turn a switch when he saw a bulb light up. He asked for nothing more than to have something else to occupy his time.

Dom Bruylants next published his *Oraisons du Missel Romain.* This is an invaluable tool, as I know from my own experience. Later on, when he became director of *Questions liturgiques et paroissiales,* he established the Center of Liturgical Documentation with its constantly updated bibliographical file. He also undertook an edition of the episcopal blessings which, thanks to Dom Eugene Moeller, just appeared in *Corpus Christianorum.*

Dom Bruylants died suddenly a few years ago in the room next to mine without my knowing it. He had returned late from Rome, very tired out by a meeting of the *Consilium.* I didn't hear him come in, and I'm sure he didn't cry out. He was found lying peacefully on his side. He was waiting to die. He had serious heart trouble and told me he expected to die in his fifties. It was a great loss for the abbey.

On the international scene the greatest worker of my generation is without doubt the Austrian Jesuit Joseph Jungmann. He began his scholarly career in 1925 with a thesis on the place of Christ in the eucharistic prayer. He then published numerous articles in the *Zeitschrift für katolische Theologie* before composing his major work, *The Mass of the Roman Rite (Missarum Sollemnia),* which was translated into several languages. It is a summa of everything that can be said about the history of the Mass. He told me that he had some difficulties with certain translations. For instance, he had used the expression "Festgedank" (idea of the feast). Since this word is not found in the dictionary, the nuns in charge of the

Italian translation were mistaken about the meaning of "Fest" and translated the word by "pensiero fisso" (fixed idea). Father Jungmann is a modest man who gives his opinion calmly without ever insisting, but he is listened to and can be considered the guide of the German liturgical movement. His influence on Vatican II and on the liturgical reform has been considerable.

Father Jungmann is not an isolated individual. He belongs to that generation of scholars who for half a century have broadened our understanding of the sources of tradition and have given us a better understanding of the liturgy's meaning. I cannot list them all—I can mention only those with whom I had personal contact.

The oldest of those who are still alive is, I believe, Father John-Michael Hanssens. He is the first tenured professor to teach the liturgy course at the Gregorian University. I don't know the exact date of his appointment, but I do know he had the position in 1930 because it was as professor there that he introduced himself to the liturgical congress held that year at Antwerp. He was welcomed by Dom Kreps who believed (you wouldn't know why) that a professor from the Gregorian who had a germanic name could only be German. So he spoke to him in the language of Goethe. Father Hanssens responded in German, and the conversation continued in that language till the moment Father Hanssens ventured to ask Dom Kreps where he was from. "From Antwerp," he replied. "Me too," said Father Hanssens. The conversation then continued in the purest Antwerpian dialect. Father Hanssens is a conscientious worker. He firmly believes in Dom Quentin's textual criticism method, but it seems to me he didn't always use it carefully. When he edited the works of Amalarius of Metz, I pointed out to him that his stemmas (trees of manuscript interrelationships) didn't correspond to the choice he made from the textual variants. He replied that these stemmas did not entirely represent his thought, but they had been moved about by an employee of the Vatican printing press and he had not wanted to sadden this fine man. I don't believe he had any more success with the evidence of the *Apostolic Tradition,* but we owe to him several introductory volumes about the oriental liturgies which are a rich mine of information. I regret that he did not finish this work.

The greatest liturgist in England was Dom Gregory Dix, a monk of the Anglican Abbey of Nashdom who, unfortunately, left us so soon. He is the author of the first critical edition of Hippolytus' *Apostolic Tradition.* Later on I had to criticize and correct him, but I admit that I owe him much. His method was basically sound, but his weakness was in having to trust the English translators of the oriental languages. Before the war his magazine articles prepared the way for his great work *The Shape of the Liturgy*. This attempt to trace the development of the eucharistic liturgy had enormous success, and I acknowledge that it contains new ideas and perceptive insights, but I have strong reservations about some of its daring hypotheses. I never met Dom Gregory Dix, but I corresponded with him.

In the field of oriental studies two German Benedictines should be mentioned. The first is Dom Odilo Heiming of Maria Laach, the current director of the *Archiv für Liturgiewissenschaft* and of the *Liturgiegeschichtliche Quellen und Forschungen*. Dom Heiming was a pupil of Anton Baumstark, but he kept his distance from the risky hypotheses of his professor. He was not exclusively an orientalist since he also knew Western sources very well, especially those of the Ambrosian liturgy. He kindly accepted for his series my edition of the *Apostolic Tradition*. I spent a month at Maria Laach finishing this edition, and Dom Heiming placed himself at my service. I remain heartily grateful to him.

Another pupil of Baumstark was Dom Jerome Engberding, a monk of the Abbey of Coesfeld, who became director of the review *Oriens Christianus*. His erudition was remarkable, but his judgment was less sure than Dom Heiming's.

The Abbey of Solesmes in France has always been a center for liturgical studies, but its specialty has been Gregorian Chant and musical paleography. And yet some years before the war there was an editor of the *Paléographie musicale* who turned his attention to the texts that were sung, no longer to their melodies alone. This was Dom Hesbert, who published the *Antiphonale Sextuplex*. By letter he engaged in controversy with Dom Kreps, although they were not personally acquainted. In 1940 Dom Hesbert was mobilized as an artillery captain, and he was part of the army corps that was taken captive by the German pincer movement in Northern France. Taken prisoner, Dom Hesbert escaped—not a very difficult feat. At that time I was chaplain at the Lille military hospital, and I saw thousands of prisoners walk along the rue Nationale without any guards. Dom Hesbert found some civilian clothes and a bicycle and then started pedaling in the direction of Belgium. One fine morning he arrived at the door of Mont César and introduced himself to a priest who was going out: "I'm Dom

Hesbert of Solesmes." The other replied: "And I'm Dom Kreps of Mont César." Dom Hesbert spent some time at Mont César, but he was no longer there when I returned from Lille. I met him only later on in Paris.

If you wish to make an assessment of what occurred between the two world wars, you notice that the movement clearly gained ground. From then on it was supported by quality scholarly research. Likewise, it spread widely in all Catholic countries, except Ireland. An Irishman who replied to a questionnaire about the liturgical movement said: "The history of the liturgical movement in Ireland is as simple as that of the snake: there have never been any snakes in Ireland." In 1915 I attended a funeral in Ireland. I was told it was the only occasion when the Mass was sung. All the clergy of the neighboring parishes were brought in, and all twenty of them were present to roar out the Requiem Mass. It was appalling. I believe things have changed since then. The Abbey of Glenstal, a foundation of Maredsous, is today a center of the liturgical apostolate, and there were six or seven exceptionally qualified Irish students of mine at the Institut Supérieur de Liturgie in Paris.

Some bishops, especially in Belgium, took things into their own hands and set up diocesan commissions, but I don't believe there were any national organizations at that time, much less any international ones. Furthermore, the liturgical movement had not yet become reformist. This doesn't mean that everything looked perfect or that there was nothing to change, but on the pastoral level we made the best of the traditional liturgy. Everyone knew that a reform could come only from Rome, and we observed the law.

What was Rome's attitude toward the liturgical movement? It was, I think, purely negative. I cannot recall any encouraging action or gesture, and the timid initiatives taken were received rather cooly. This was the case for the dialogue Mass. According to the rubrics responding to the priest was the task of the acolyte; and strictly speaking, the people could respond along with the acolyte. Likewise, the singing of the *Benedictus* verse was joined to that of the *Sanctus* in conformity with the *Roman Missal:* a decree was imposed pushing the *Benedictus* verse back after the consecration. Attempts to renew the shape of the liturgical vestments, especially the chasuble, were hardly appreciated. The Congregation of Rites entrenched itself behind a narrow rubricism, positing the principle that what was not explicitly permitted was forbidden.

The reform started by Pius X wasn't buried, only shelved. I saw the beginnings of a revision of the Roman Pontifical: it was a collation of texts from the last typical edition and the editions of the sixteenth century. This was not a reform in depth. Besides, the work was never completed.

The years following the war of 1914-1918 were a period of rebirth and progress for the liturgical movement, but a decline was now underway. The arrival of Hitler slowed down scholarly work in Germany. The progressive extension of World War II would stop everything and, without doubt, for a long time.

At least, this is what I was thinking. Yet even before the end of that deluge of fire and blood a message of hope reached me, like Noah's dove with its olive branch. In this case the dove was a young Dominican (I've forgotten his name) who came from Paris to propose that I collaborate in a new series launched by Éditions du Cerf, that is, the *Sources chrétiennes.* He asked me to take charge of editing the *Apostolic Tradition,* and he insisted on the urgency of this book since this text was fundamental for the liturgical movement which had just been born in France. This is how I learned that two Dominicans, Père Roguet and Père Duployé, had founded the Centre de Pastorale Liturgique with the help of Abbé Martimort, a young professor at the Toulouse School of Theology. I agreed to prepare the edition. Perhaps this was imprudent since I hadn't gauged all the difficulties in the project. Furthermore, circumstances were hardly favorable. The abbey had suffered a severe bombardment in 1944, and it was just beginning to undergo repairs. The library had been stored in the basement because the "V-1s" kept passing over our city on their way to Antwerp. The Jesuits had taken the same precaution. As for the university library, only the walls were intact, and almost all the books had been reduced to ashes during the blaze of 1940. Once I dug the essential books out of the basement, a task not without difficulty, I set to work. Very quickly I realized that it would take years to do a scholarly job. In fact, it took eighteen years, till 1963, before my critical edition was completed. But since this text was practically beyond the reach of the French readers and since it was considered fundamental for the liturgical movement, I resigned myself to providing a provisional edition which appeared in 1946. This was my first contact with the French liturgical movement. Only in 1948 did I have direct relations with the Centre de Pastorale Liturgique de Paris.

7

The Paris Pastoral
Liturgy Center

A shift in leadership of the liturgical movement occurred after World War II. France took many initiatives to adopt effective pastoral strategies in an effort to popularize liturgical life in the church. Botte dates the commencement of his relationship with the C.P.L. (the French national pastoral center) from 1948, five years after its founding. Botte collaborated with a veritable "Who's Who" of French liturgists who eventually acquired international fame: A.-M. Roguet, Antoine Chavasse, Aimée-Georges Martimort, Jean Daniélou, Louis Bouyer, Pierre-Marie Gy, and Irenée Dalmais. Several times Botte comments on the French penchant for allowing political stances and problems to impact on liturgical renewal. It was during this same period that the Liturgical Weeks in the United States began their work of popularizing the agenda of the liturgical movement. (Tr.)

T HE CENTRE DE PASTORALE LITURGIQUE DE PARIS (C.P.L.) made contact with Mont César at the end of the war. Dom Capelle and Dom Anselm Robeyns had already taken part in sessions organized by the C.P.L. It was only in 1948, after a few misunderstandings, that I was personally invited.

The directors of the C.P.L. decided to sponsor at Vanves a study session on the liturgy of the sick. To speak about the anointing of the sick they invited the best specialist on the topic, Abbé Antoine Chavasse, then professor at the Lyons School of Theology. But he noticed on the program the name of someone he did not wish to meet, or more exactly, someone whom he wished not to meet. Abbé Philippeau, an eccentric, was an assistant at Saint Louis d'Antin church in Paris and spent all his mornings in the confessional and all his afternoons in the manuscript room of the Bibliothèque Nationale. Thus he had acquired a somewhat chaotic erudition, but had no well-founded training and—what is worse—he lacked all common sense and his deductions generally ended with some preposterous hypotheses. Well, he published an article on extreme unction in which he offered three opinions: that of the traditional theologians, that of the modernists, and his own, which evidently was the good one. The modernist position was the one represented by Abbé Chavasse. It's understandable how the latter did not want to engage in controversy with this odd character. He refused to attend. Dom Capelle was then asked to treat the problem of the anointing of the sick, but he was not disposed to accept. During the preceding session of the C.P.L. he had a serious tiff with Père Roguet about the Mass. Later on this was settled—Père Roguet admitted honestly that he was mistaken. But at that particular moment Dom Capelle wanted to put some distance between himself and the C.P.L. Still, a pure and simple refusal could have seemed a gesture of breaking-off, all the more so that the C.P.L. was visibly embarrassed. One morning Dom Capelle waited for me after the conventual Mass and asked me whether I would please take his place. I answered that if I were invited by the directors of the C.P.L. I would accept. I had never studied this subject in particular, but I had all the time needed to get ready. I received an invitation, and thus it was that I took part for the first time in a session of the C.P.L., with the rank of a substitute.

At this session I once again met an old acquaintance, Dom Lambert Beauduin. Exiled from Belgium in the wake of the difficulties he had at Amay over ecumenism, he was living at Chatou in the diocese of Versailles. The founders of the C.P.L. had taken him as an advisor, and they always had affectionate reverence for him. He gave a paper on viaticum.

We also had the famous talk of Père Philippeau. The poor man condensed all his erudition into a voluminous dossier which was impossible to unpack in one hour. He wanted to deliver as much as possible and, as time went by, he spoke faster and faster. It became quite a marathon and, since the speaker's diction was quite peculiar, the whole affair turned out to be quite amusing. The audience was evidently enjoying itself, and everyone was in a good mood when Abbé Martimort succeeded in stopping the inundation of words.

I retained one typical fact from this session. Among the forty priests on hand more than half were totally unaware that the *Roman Ritual* contained a section on visiting the sick, with Gospel readings and special prayers. This was true since most used abbreviated diocesan rituals which omitted this section. My memory of this is all the more striking since a little afterwards a curate from Walloon Brabant came to visit me and asked advice about a sick worker in his parish who was almost always bedridden. The priest went to see him regularly, but the sick man always acted disagreeably. Then, one day he found him completely changed. What had happened? He gave no other reason than a visit from the Jehovah's Witnesses who read the Gospel to him. The sick man simply said, "Father, why haven't you ever spoken to me about all this?" The curate was disturbed and came to ask me if it was permitted to read the Gospel in that way to the sick. I reassured him by referring him to the *Roman Ritual.* What a strange aberration among the Catholic clergy to replace the word of God by an empty chat.

These work sessions prepared for the big sessions of Versailles where three or four hundred priests were present. Such preparatory gatherings were held at Vanves, in the Paris suburbs, at the Priory of Sainte-Bathilde of the missionary Benedictines. The house was rather new, very pleasant, with a big garden. The meetings were private, by invitiation only. More than once I saw Abbé Martimort conduct to the door certain interlopers who wanted to force their way in. Invitations were sent to about forty people who were able to contribute something to the discussions. There was a wide sampling of representatives of the French clergy: parish priests, Catholic Action chaplains, religious from all orders. There were also some lay people who were very involved in Catholic Action. Among them I especially remember André Cruiziat, whose solid common sense I always admired.

The C.P.L. had a special status. It was an independent structure: independent, first of all, from the Dominicans in spite of appearances since Éditions du Cerf (owned by the Dominicans) loaned it office space at the beginning and took care of its publications; also independent of the bishops except, of course, for the *Imprimatur* required for publications. The C.P.L. did not depend on the Episcopal Commission of Pastoral Action and of Liturgy which at that time was presided over by Archbishop Martin of Rouen. Still, it wanted to work in full accord with this commission, but it was never an official structure. There were two directors. One was Abbé Martimort, or rather Canon Martimort since he had just been made a Canon of Chartres by Bishop Harscouët. The other was the Dominican Père Roguet. They shared responsibility. But Père Roguet, who was a Master in Theology, was aware that his strictly scholastic training had poorly prepared him for running things, and so he was happy to let his colleague be more visible.

In practice, Canon Martimort always presided over the sessions. He knew how to sum up different positions, list problems, and bring the debate back to its proper subject. Good work was accomplished. Only one thing somewhat bothered me: the schedule was never respected. It seems that few speakers know how to judge in advance how long their talk will be. And yet, it's not difficult. I have a very simple system. A page typed with average spacing and sufficiently wide margins takes two minutes to read out loud. If you have an hour, you must never go beyond thirty pages. It's better to have only twenty- five so as to allow for pauses or interruptions.

The debates were sometimes quite lively. Some pastors in working-class parishes complained that the liturgical technicians were not on the wavelength of their own pastoral anguish. I don't believe this is exact. I've always tried, in my own way, to listen with interest as the pastors explained their problems. But I wasn't there to show my emotion, and I had another anguish: that of seeing priests of undeniable generosity bury themselves in politics and mix up the great social upheaval to come with the coming of the Lord. When I heard a priest speak about his Marxist ideal, it wasn't for me to judge him. To what extent can the Marxist ideal be harmonized with the Gospel ideal? I don't know, and it's for each of us to judge according to individual conscience. But what I am sure of is that the priest's mission is to preach the Gospel of Jesus Christ and not the Gospel of Marx. The problem came up in regard to a feast for workers. Could we incorporate this holiday into the Christian liturgy? I had given a paper on the dispensation of salvation, and I had to answer the question. I said no. The liturgy is the celebration of the dispensation of salvation, that is, of the action of God in the world, and not the glorification of human realities, regardless of how respectable they might be, such as work, motherhood, or fatherhood. Like all human realities these can be sanctified; they are not the object of worship. You can bless a plane or a locomotive, but a feast of the railroads or of aviation cannot be introduced into the liturgical year. Does this mean that pastors have to ignore the existing feast of workers? The church can share in it, just as it shares in other secular holidays, such as national holidays, and on this occasion celebrate Mass for the workers. It is true that these human festivals would draw to church people who are not interested in the death or the birth of Christ. But making people believe that the church can give work the same meaning and the same values as the Marxists is either a fraud or a perversion of the Gospel. Of course Christians have the duty, like other people, to improve the human condition by their work—no one doubts this. But is this the Kingdom of God which Christ preached?

My fondest memories come from the sessions devoted to the priesthood. The first of these two meetings had been announced when the crisis of the worker priests broke in France. Wasn't it too burning an issue, all the more so for the way the issue went far beyond the liturgical sphere? The organizers had the courage not to back off, and they were right. The problems had to be listed, and a start had to be made from a doctrinal basis. Next we would see what had been the history of how priests lived. My role was to study the priesthood according to the ordination rites in the West and East. At the end of the session we realized that we had not covered all aspects of the topic, and some important points were left to be treated in greater depth. Canon Boulard, the Chaplain General of Rural Catholic Action, was especially impressed by the collegial nature of the priesthood as expounded in my paper. He asked that this aspect be studied in a following session. I then treated the question not from the liturgical but from the patristic point of view. At the end of the session a new method of approaching the problem was proposed. Traditional theology started out with the simple priest who had received power to consecrate the eucharist. The priest was essentially the person who was able to offer sacrifice. But then, who was the bishop? A study of tradition led us to another method: start with the bishop, the successor of the apostles and the head of the *presbyterium*. The pastor of Saint-Sulpice, Abbé Lesourd, told me he was present at the interview of the Archbishop of Paris with his worker priests. The Cardinal began by quoting the beginning of the address in the *Pontifical:* "Sacerdos oportet benedicere" ("The priest's duty is to bless"). Was this really what should have been said at that time? Or wouldn't he have been better to remind them of the solidarity of the *presbyterium* with its bishop?

Thus it was by accident—at the request of Canon Boulard—that I was led to study collegiality. My second paper was published in *Irénikon.* Afterwards, I was asked to speak at an ecumenical meeting held at Chevetogne. The text appeared in the volume of essays *Le Concile et les conciles.*

The two Vanves meetings went well, and it was decided to publish all the reports in one volume of the series *Lex orandi.* This is when the difficulties began. Various French Dominicans had experienced some difficulties and the General of their order decided that all articles appearing in Dominican journals and collections had to be censored in Rome. As a result my two papers were submitted to a Roman Dominican. To my utter dismay he wanted to impose some inept corrections. Clearly, the censor did not understand French. My article in *Irénikon* had been read and approved by Bishop Charue of Namur who was extremely interested in the question. I categorically refused to change anything, and I threatened to withdraw my articles and publish them independently with a preface that would say why they were not appearing in the collection. The General of the Dominicans gave in.

I regularly attended these work sessions, and I feel they steered the French liturgical movement in a good direction. The C.P.L. wanted to gather all the documentation necessary for reflection in common. First of all, this was to understand tradition. They were not satisfied with a second-hand popularization, but requested studies of the problems from specialists like Dom Capelle, Abbé Chavasse, Père Daniélou, and Père Bouyer. To cover the pastoral point of view they invited priests from different settings: pastors of city, country, and worker parishes; chaplains of Catholic Action; and worker priests. I was impressed by the variety of pastoral experiences. It was impossible to find solutions to all cases, but the C.P.L. didn't try to supply infallible recipes—it wanted to give principles and directions that could be followed.

As for the general meetings held at Versailles, I went only twice.

Their spirit was different. There was no opportunity for starting a discussion with an audience of three or four hundred persons. Results from the work sessions were presented, followed by round-table group discussions.

At the first Versailles meeting I attended I spoke about the presidential prayer. I did a history of euchology: improvisation, prepared compositions, fixed formulas, compilations. From the fourth century on freedom of composition was limited. Saint Augustine was already complaining about incompetent windbags who were composing prayer formulas. I put the audience on guard against the temptation of improvising formulas which followed contemporary tastes and could be understood by the un-educated man-in-the- street. You don't make a Christian liturgy for people who know nothing of the Old and very little of the New Testaments. Without a renewal of catechesis and preaching, liturgical reform is doomed to failure.

At the second Versailles meeting I considered baptismal texts. There was a liturgical ritual prepared by the diocesan commission of Paris, but it contained a good number of conflicting meanings. I knew one of the members of this commission who admitted there were some unintelligible passages, but a translation had to be provided.

People began talking about a liturgical reform—I'll return to this later on—but the C.P.L. was very prudent and warned against untimely initiatives. At any rate, nothing could be done without the authorization of the bishops who could permit certain ex-periments. The C.P.L. has always been a restraining organization and tried to ward off anarchy. However, it must be admitted that it did not find favor with Rome. Later on I will return to this point in connection with the Institut Supérieur de Liturgie.

My contacts with the C.P.L. led me to become acquainted with a good number of persons with whom I would continue to work: the directors of the C.P.L., of course, but also Père Gy and Père Dalmais, who later on would be my collaborators at the I.S.L. They were then young theologians who were just finishing their studies. One of the most constant members of our public was the pastor of Millau, who became bishop of Saint-Flour, then arch-bishop of Rheims, and who today is archbishop of Paris, namely, Cardinal Marty.

In a more general way, these contacts led me to know the French better. Until then, my experience was limited to a stay of six months spent in Lille as chaplain of the military hospital and, at the same time, curate in Sacred Heart Parish. Since 1948 my visits to France became more frequent, and I was able to observe the French from up close, with friendliness, but also with a certain critical sense. This enables one to understand many things, even in regard to liturgy. The Frenchman is stricken with a political virus. One must be either on the left or on the right. There can be no plain center: there's a center-right and a center-left, and this makes itself felt in the most diverse spheres. I had an argument with a French confrere over a question of textual criticism. I reproached him for using a majority method and received an indignant reply. He protested that he was an enemy of any majority system, that universal suffrage was an absurdity, that he had always been for Marshal (Pétain) and not the General (de Gaulle). I answered that, not being French, I worried as little about the Marshal as about the General. Politics also influences judgments on liturgical reform. The more to the right you are, the less you like it. One evening I had a meal with the people of the Action Française. There I learned that there's nothing good in these (liturgical) reforms. But when you get close to the center-left, these reforms become inadequate.

I hope my French friends—there are lots of them on both the right and the left—won't be offended by these remarks. France has always extended a warm welcome to people, and I like the French a lot. But it's precisely because I like them that I sometimes allow myself to smile kindly at their foibles.

8

Translation Problems

The proven skills and expertise of Dom Botte as an orientalist familiar with textual analysis show through brilliantly in this chapter. The task of rendering ancient prayer texts and biblical passages into the vernacular—at a time when the liturgy was celebrated entirely in Latin—demanded a resourceful use of erudition and a fair amount of courage, attitudes still needed today as we work on new forms of linguistic expression and symbolism in liturgy. Botte predicated his collaboration in the projects of the C.P.L. on the conviction that "the barrier of Latin contributed to keeping Christians from active participation in the sacred mysteries." (Tr.)

P ROBLEMS OF TRANSLATION AROSE from the beginning of Christianity. Even the revelation of the Old Testament was able to spread through the Mediterranean world only thanks to the Septuagint, a Greek version of the Bible which later became the Bible of the Christians. Once the message of Jesus had passed the borders of Palestine it also had to adopt the form of the Greek Gospels. You could say that Greek was the official language of the universal church. And yet, to the extent that the Gospel moved deeper into different regions, the need for written translations into different languages was felt. Thus, we find already from the second century onward biblical versions in Latin, Syriac, Coptic, then Armenian, Georgian, and Ethiopian. Liturgy underwent the same evolution; and naturally so since the Bible was the very basis of liturgy. Worship services were spent reading the Old Testament, the Gospels, the writings of the Apostles. The psalter was the song book of the congregation. The church of the first centuries never dreamed of celebrating the mysteries of Christ in a tongue unknown to the people. On the contrary, as soon as it found an adequately evolved language which had a written form, it hastened to adopt it. If Latin became the liturgical language, it is not because it was a sacred language, but because it was the living language of the Roman people.

Still, drafted texts were fixed once for all by writing, and they could no longer change, whereas the spoken tongue evolved and dissolved into dialects according to regions. A time came when the liturgical texts were no longer understood by the people. The same phenomenon occurred in the East, especially from the time Arabic was imposed in many parts of the region by Islam's victories. In the West Latin was the only cultural language. Neither the Celts nor the Germans possessed a system of writing before the fourth century. Latin was not only the liturgical language; it remained the scholarly world's tongue and this produced the unity of Western civilization. This was still the situation at the beginning of the sixteenth century when the Reformation made its appearance.

Among the Reformation's claims the one which sounds the most legitimate is certainly that of reading Scripture in the vernacular at worship. But it's not all that simple. The Reformers had broken with tradition. Who would verify the exactness of the translations and the legitimacy of the interpretations based on them? As for a liturgical reform by the new theologians, it included the destruction of the Catholic faith. The Council of Trent reacted energetically and retained the use of Latin in order to preserve intact the deposit of faith contained in the prayer of the church.

It is certain that the barrier of Latin contributed to keeping Christians from active participation in the sacred mysteries. When the liturgical movement began, its promoters understood that the first thing to do was to reestablish contact through translations. Thus, Dom Beauduin began publishing *La vie liturgique* which put into the faithful's hands the texts read in the liturgy and translations of them. Then came full missals, which rapidly attained wide circulation. We must acknowledge that the remedy, even though imperfect, was effective. After World War II missals were on the increase: besides that of Dom Lefebvre, there soon was a Rural Missal, the Missal of Hautecombe, one by Dom Capelle, and another on the way which became the Missal of Père Feder.

This zeal among editors was healthy in itself, but it posed some dangers. First, it was evident that for all the best of intentions, the editors did not all have the same competence and that sometimes much was left to be desired in the accuracy of the translations. Furthermore, if the vernacular would one day be allowed in liturgical celebration, then a common text would have to be produced. The directors of the C.P.L. felt that it would be useful to coordinate and not dissipate efforts. So they proposed to work with missal editors on the translation of the central section of the missal, that is, the canon, whose text remained fixed since Saint Gregory the Great. The editors agreed to work as a team. The current abbot of Saint-André, Dom Ghesquière, represented the Missal of Dom Lefebvre; Canon Boulard, the Rural Missal; Dom Dumas, the Missal of Hautecombe; and Pères Feder and Gelineau were included for the new missal they were working on. The directors of the C.P.L. were smart to bring into the project the undisputed specialist of Christian Latin, Miss Christine Mohrmann—a better choice could not have been possible. I was invited as the author of a critical edition of the canon of the Roman Mass.

Translation work involves two operations: first of all, understanding the original text with all its nuances; and then finding the equivalent phrases in the language into which a text is to be translated. This seems very simple; in actual fact, it is very complicated.

Any understanding of an ancient liturgical text demands more than a basic, general knowledge of classical Latin. The latter has evolved like all languages and, besides, it underwent the profound influence of Christianity. On the other hand, there are differing levels of a language in the same period. The Roman canon belongs to the rhythmical oratorical prose of the fifth century, and it cannot be understood unless the rhythmic element be kept in mind. The choice of certain words may depend on the "cursus." There's no method worse than having recourse to etymology— something amateurs try so often. One must study the semantic evolution of the words. I believe we did some thorough work from the philological point of view, and this was a help to translators in other languages.

Regarding the translation itself, we agreed to make it as accurate as possible, without attempting adaptations to one setting or another. So we kept an oratorical style which rendered the same tone as the original. In this regard I would point out a bias frequently attributed to modern French: it has to consist of short sentences, one after the other. I believe this bespeaks a mix-up between linguistic levels and literary genres. Cicero did not compose periods to order lunch, but he made them in his speeches. Isn't there any difference in French between conversational and oratorical style, so that the listener today is unable to follow a sentence more than three lines long? I did a study of modern orators, for example, in the speeches of Bishop Chevrot. There are sentences of seven lines or more, with "whichs" and "whos" that are perfectly clear. But the most striking example is that of General de Gaulle: I'm not qualified to judge his politics because I'm not French, but without being excessively partisan I admire him as an orator. You might say that he was a man of another generation, but when he made a speech in 1968 or 1969 he was perfectly understood by people of all ages. François Mauriac also knew how to put together a sentence. He too was a man of another generation, but his readers weren't all septuagenarians. When he was on vacation and wasn't writing his weekly column the sales of *Figaro littéraire* went down by fifty percent. Were those who didn't buy it all old people? I believe that there are fewer and fewer people able to speak and write that way, but those who do are always understood.

Our translation was published in an issue of *La Maison-Dieu* with explanatory notes, and it was well received. So we decided to continue and undertake a translation of the rest of the Ordinary of the Mass. The same method was followed in a series of short meetings two or three days long. This led to the publication of *L'Ordinaire de la Messe* under the names of Miss Mohrmann and myself.

Some of the French were offended at a French translation published under the names of a Belgian and a Dutchwoman. Just between ourselves, book sales were the determining factor. Experience shows that an anonymous collection doesn't sell. Since we needed authors' names, it was natural to choose those collaborators who enhanced the volume by the scholarly notes they had contributed; but the preface stated clearly that the translation was the work of a team. Since the names of the team members were listed, everyone could see that most of them were Frenchmen from different parts of France. Just by the way, I must say that Miss Mohrmann, though Dutch, is most capable of catching the nuances of modern French. We had gone to eat together in a restaurant on rue Saint Dominique in Paris. The menu indicated "pommes Pont-Neuf." None of us knew what that meant, except Miss Mohrmann who explained they were simply fried potatoes, called "Pont-Neuf" because of their long shape. I always avoided choosing between what is said south of the Loire and what is said north of the Loire [the different ways of cooking either with oil or with butter].

After the Ordinary of the Mass, the translation commission took on another job. In 1957 France received the privilege of a ritual with one part giving prayers translated into French. As I mentioned earlier, this work had already been done by a team from the diocese of Paris. The results were hardly satisfactory, and a revision was entrusted to the commission formed by the C.P.L.

After the ritual came a translation of the biblical pericopes of the Sunday Masses. The commission was officially established by the French episcopate. Presiding was the then bishop of Saint-Jean-de-Maurienne (and now of Tours), Bishop Ferrand. Two exegetes were added to the team: Père Gelin, professor at the School of Theology at Lyons, and Canon Renard, to represent the *Bible of Lille*. Since Miss Mohrmann didn't have any special expertise in biblical studies, she no longer was a member of the commission. The problems were entirely different from those raised by the liturgical texts.

You might wonder whether it wasn't possible to choose an existing translation. We would have had to find one that was superior to all the others, one which would work especially well when read out loud. Now, the polls we had taken showed us that this translation did not exist. The *Jerusalem Bible* in particular had some big drawbacks. The different biblical books were given to competent collaborators who frequently had diverse methods, so that parallel texts looked dissimilar when translated. The director of the project, Père Chifflot, was entirely aware of this defect and tried to correct it in subsequent editions, but the work of standardization was far from complete. So we decided to look at the pericopes ourselves.

The first problem to arise concerned the basic text. Should we work from the Latin text of the Roman Missal or from the original? The question is not so simple, and does not let itself get locked into a dilemma because, if you opt for the original text, another question arises: where is the original text? It is a bit naive to believe that our manuals of the New Testament Greek texts present us with the original text in all its purity or that it is always superior to the basic text of the Vulgate. In fact, the Greek texts are very diverse. What is called the "received text," that is, the one in the first printed editions, relies on late manuscripts and is less reliable than the one supposed by the Vulgate. At the end of the nineteenth century it was dethroned by a textual form derived from earlier manuscripts but which are still far from the originals. They represent a recension of the fourth century. It is the basis for our manual editions, but commentators are not always in agreement about its value. For the last thirty years textual criticism has been in full evolution for two reasons. The first is the discovery of more ancient manuscripts, especially on papyrus, which furnish new data. The second is increased attention paid to ancient versions and to patristic quotations. We were not about to undertake scholarly research: a liturgical lectionary is not to give the latest state of textual criticism which is liable to become the next-to-latest in a few years' time. This is how we went about our work. As our basic text we used the Greek version of the current edition of Nestle and compared it with the Vulgate. When the latter presupposed a different Greek text we checked to see whether this variant had solid support in the Greek tradition. If it did, then we retained it. If, on the other hand, we had a Latin peculiarity, then we stuck to the Greek. This isn't the method I'd follow if I were to make a critical edition, but it seemed to be the most reasonable one, given our goal.

As for translation methods, our primary objective was exactness and accuracy. Since the majority of the commission's members were neither experts in Hellenism nor professional exegetes, I asked that we invite a professor of sacred Scripture. Père Pierre Grelot, a professor at the Institut Catholique in Paris, was chosen. Naturally we consulted some printed translations and commentaries. We paid attention to two points. The first was readability: the translation had to lend itself to reading aloud. Many pericopes were tested in parishes before being printed. The second point was harmony of vocabulary.

I'll not claim that this lectionary was a masterpiece beyond all criticism. I only want to point out that it wasn't something thrown together by a few amateurs. From a critical point of view I believe that the presence of Père Grelot and myself was an adequate guarantee of this. Regarding the French idiom, there was among others Père Roguet, an experienced radio speaker and someone who ought to know twentieth-century French well. There was also a collaborator of the Rural Missal (whose name I've forgotten) who had a certain knack for translation. When he assured me that a particular expression would be perfectly understood, I could trust him completely.

How was the lectionary received? Very poorly by an issue of the *Témoignage chrétien*. I don't know if this represented the general or the average opinion of the French clergy. I'm even less sure of the good sense of this magazine's editors. On occasion I've read some pretty astounding things in it. I remember a little article that criticized the traditional image of eternal rest. What an error: joy—on the contrary—is work. When there's no salary, there's no bread in the house. You can see the conclusions that can be drawn from this mix-up between rest and unemployment. But then you wonder why workers don't demand a work week of fifty hours and hold off retirement till they are eighty. If workers would have read the article, they would have laughed at a priest telling them about the joy of work, because it was an avant-garde priest who wrote the article. You could see the outfit's attitude. The priests who criticized the lectionary were of the same kind. They wanted startling translations, modern adaptations of the old worn-out Gospels. We were referred to the example of Père Godin's Missal. I remember one of these adaptations. It concerned the Epistle to the Galatians where Saint Paul states that the heir, not yet of age, is no different from a slave. Père Godin transposed terms by saying that the son of a factory owner had no more rights than a worker. I don't know if this is entirely exact, but I am sure that Père Godin—who wrote for the Young Christian Workers— would never have dreamed of imposing this translation on all of France. Besides, one would have to switch settings and speak of the farmer's son in a country milieu. The drawback to these adaptations is that they do not apply to everyone and quickly go out of style. The apostles once became "militants." Who would still dare to use this word today?

A difficulty arises from the usage of language. There are words and expressions which are found only in translations and which ought to be banished. But there are also essential words that are part of the Christian vocabulary—I'll take two: justice and mercy.

The traditional translation of "Happy are those who suffer persecution for justice's sake" has been criticized with the excuse that the word "justice" today evokes the police and the courts. So it is proposed that justice be replaced by "good cause." This doesn't appear very sensible to me. Words have precise meaning only in context. Who would imagine that people would be persecuted for the police's sake? Besides, there is a biblical notion of justice, and I defy anyone to translate the Bible without using this word. Its use presents us with a fine opportunity for explaining what justice and just persons are in the Bible, but the "good cause" doesn't mean anything.

As for "mercy," this does not enjoy the favor of certain translators either. A few years ago a priest told me that love and not mercy was spoken about in preaching. I've been noticing that translations of the Mass prayers into French make use of the term "love" in a way that appears abnormal to me; yet, mercy is not to be mistaken for love. Mercy is the feeling we have toward an unfortunate person: that is the meaning of *eleos* in Greek. It is impossible to translate the Bible without using this and related words. I can't translate "Beati misericordes" by "Blessed are the lovers." And you needn't know anything of the writings of Saint Paul to think you can translate his message and omit the mercy of God.

It's not by adaptations and whims that the problem of biblical translations will be solved. You can't have translations that are so clear that they are perfectly understood at first sight, without explanations. Only people who have no biblical background are under this illusion. To be understood the Scriptures have to be read, re-read, meditated upon, and explained. This is what happened in ancient times. But we begin by having a desire for faithful translations, out of respect for the word of God.

9

The Movement Broadens

Linkage to and cross-fertilization from other renewal movements was very noticeable in the liturgical movement after World War II. Botte attests to the benefits liturgists reaped from progress in patristic studies, biblical research, and the awareness of Judaism's cultural legacy to Christianity. A strong impetus in favor of the "pastoral value of the liturgy" came from Pope Pius XII's encyclical *Mediator Dei* (1947). The theological implications of the encyclical confirmed the emphasis found in American liturgical circles to assure linkage between worship and social commitment.

A practical consequence of the encyclical's bow in the direction of reform was a series of international study meetings of scholars held at regular intervals in the 1950s. The proceedings of the last of these gatherings (Assisi, 1956) were published in the United States as a supplement to *Worship* magazine and became known as the *Assisi Papers*. These proved to be a watershed volume for Americans interested in the aims of the liturgical movement. All the meetings provided forums for delving into the sources of liturgical tradition and for analyzing pastoral needs—which would make Vatican II's Constitution on the Sacred Liturgy the best prepared document of the Council. (Tr.)

I HAVE DEVOTED A GOOD DEAL OF TIME to discussing the work of the Pastoral Liturgy Center in Paris. And yet, it is only a detail in the story of the liturgical movement after World War II. To understand the rapid development of the movement we must broaden our horizon. First of all, you must take note that the liturgical movement benefited from other movements which returned to the sources. I have already alluded to the collection *Sources chrétiennes*. The aim of this undertaking was to make available to a large part of the Christian reading public works that were practically unfamiliar to them. Only specialists were able to consult critical editions and, besides, the barrier of Latin and Greek limited the number of readers. Among the volumes planned by the program there were, of course, texts of major importance for the liturgy. This is why I was called upon, as I have mentioned, to edit the *Apostolic Tradition* of Hippolytus. I was next asked to translate the *De sacramentis* and the *De mysteriis* of Saint Ambrose. I first suggested that a younger confrere take on this translation. He accepted, but rather quickly became discouraged. I can understand why. The text established in the eighteenth century by the Benedictines of Saint Maur is clearly faulty. Likewise, a critical edition was being prepared, but the date of publication remained uncertain. I decided to do a better edition by using a group of manuscripts that were unknown to the Maurists. Only in the second edition was I able to adopt, with some corrections, the critical text of Père Faller. Later on other volumes related to the liturgy appeared in the collection, for example, the *De baptismo* of Tertullian edited by Père Refoulé, and the *Baptismal Catecheses* of Saint John Chrysostom by Père Wenger.

A return to sacred Scripture could be seen as a parallel to this return to the Church Fathers. Certainly the renewal of biblical studies goes back much further: at the end of the nineteenth century Leo XIII wished to encourage study of the Bible. Unfortunately, the Modernist crisis and the anti-Modernist reaction blocked everything for a good number of years. The group created for directing scriptural studies, the Biblical Commission, resembled a car equipped with powerful brakes but lacking a motor. A series of decrees set the limits that were to be observed so that work always ended up at roadblocks, and people felt they were going around in circles. For a long time the École Biblique in Jerusalem was under suspicion, and its founder, Père Lagrange, was never able to publish certain commentaries which would have unleashed stormy reactions from the Index. As far as the Biblicum in Rome goes, it is no surprise that it avoided burning issues. The masterpiece of its director, Père Fonck, was a study on biblical flora. Dom de Bruyne ended his book review of this work in the *Revue bénédictine* on this cool note: "All that remains now is to study the biblical fauna"!

The encyclical *Spiritus paraclitus* of Benedict XV in 1920 was a timid opening toward biblical criticism, but you had to wait till 1943 to be in a position to speak of a liberation by Pius XII's encyclical *Divino afflante*. This shows that the faithful were not reached by the biblical renewal before World War II. The Bible remained for them a closed book, but a few years later we encountered a radical change. We saw the publication, more or less simultaneously, of three new French language versions of the Bible: the *Jerusalem Bible*, and those of Lille and Maredsous. Publishing houses are not crazy: they make things available when there's a demand for them. Dom Celestine Charlier, a Benedictine of Maredsous, wrote a book which was deservedly successful, *La lecture chrétienne de la Bible*, and founded the magazine *Bible et vie chrétienne* for a very wide audience. Its special purpose was to help the Bible study clubs which were springing up almost everywhere. Dom Charlier is one of the last students I had when I was professor of Scripture. I had directed him toward the study of the ancient Latin versions of the Bible. He began a new edition of Pelagius' commentaries on the epistles of Saint Paul and worked on it for several years. Unfortunately, his health, always delicate, halted the completion of this scholarly undertaking.

The liturgical movement gained much from this return to the Bible by Christians. For liturgy has always been impregnated by Holy Scripture: from it liturgy has borrowed its language and has nourished itself on its substance. The screen which separated people from the liturgy came not only from the Latin, but also from ignorance of the Scriptures. It seems to me that a renewal of the liturgy is inseparable from a return to catechesis and preaching based on the Bible.

With the biblical renewal came an increased interest in Judaism. Christianity was originally a Jewish sect, and it cannot be understood without a knowledge of the setting in which it was born. This is true in general and also in the realm of prayer. Christian liturgy has its roots in the same soil as Jewish liturgy, and knowing the condition of the latter at the time of the apostles makes a difference, although the sources of rabbinical Judaism are not accessible to everyone. To study them in a critical way requires very special scholarly training. Amateurs will only go astray in it and lead others into error.

During my stays in Paris my headquarters was with the Pères de Sion at 68, rue Notre-Dame des Champs, where I established a friendship with a group of scholars of the *Cahiers sioniens*. I was interested in their research, and I shared in the work of the *Cahiers* by contributing articles and book reviews; but at the same time I tried to steer the work of the team toward the history of the Jewish liturgy. Thus it was that Mademoiselle Renée Bloch undertook a study of the systems of biblical readings in the synagogue liturgy. Unfortunately, she died in a plane crash. This was a great loss, not only from the perspective of the research, but also for the team's morale. I am convinced that had she not died, she would have headed off the breakup of the team. A little later another member left Paris for personal reasons and took up residence in England. This was Professor Vermès of Oxford. But the real blow came with the departure of the head of the team, Père Paul Démann. I still regard him as a friend, but I can only think with sadness of the work he could have accomplished had he remained at his post. Père Kurt Hruby is the only member of the original group still around today. He is a professor at the Institut Catholique and is one of the best specialists on the Jewish liturgy. He gives regular courses at the Institut Supérieur de Liturgie in Paris and, as will be mentioned later on, often takes part in the study weeks at Saint-Serge. I hope he will be able to form a group of competent collaborators.

Thus the liturgical movement at the end of World War II was supported by other movements which returned to the sources. However, the primary phenomenon of this period was the intervention of Pius XII in 1947 by the encyclical *Mediator Dei*. Till then the liturgical movement received but little encouragement from Rome. The liturgical reform begun by Pius X seemed to have come to a halt, and the Congregation of Rites was immobilized by rigid rubricism. Then along came the Pope to announce the spiritual and pastoral value of the liturgy. His encyclical looked like a charter granted to the liturgical movement. Some theologians wondered whether the encyclical contained a condemnation of the theories of Dom Casel. This was certainly not the principal goal of the encyclical whose essentials were eminently positive. At most, one could see in it a caution against certain interpretations of these theories. Besides, the liturgical movement as a whole did not link itself to the theology of Dom Casel.

The encyclical was received as an encouragement to the liturgical movement, and the possibility of restarting the reform begun by Pius X could be seen. As I said earlier, the liturgical movement was not at the beginning reformist in tendency. The liturgy was accepted as it was at the time, and we tried to do our best with it. This didn't keep people from seeing its defects and gaps; but we knew that a reform could come only from Rome and that poorly timed initiatives would unleash hostile reactions. The leaders of the movement acted prudently. They were happy to present critiques and theoretical desiderata without applying themselves to practical reform measures. The new situation created by *Mediator Dei* opened up more optimistic prospects. The Pope's good will was assured, but the Pope is not alone in Rome and does not always get what he wants done. A liturgical reform was not possible without the Congregation of Rites, and it is known that the Congregation has heavy machinery which requires some effort to set into motion. Waiting for it to start moving on its own would postpone the reform till far into the future. Taking the initiative without its approval would cause it to apply the brakes. So, a middle-of-the-road solution was chosen: private preparation of reform proposals to be presented to Rome by the episcopates of different countries. But to accomplish this one had to avoid dispersion of work. It was important to do the opposite and concentrate the efforts of the different groups at work. This was the origin of the international meetings.

Where did this idea come from? It sprang from the close collaboration of the Paris C.P.L. and the Liturgical Institute of Trier. In spite of its title, the latter was not a teaching institute, but a study and organizational body of the liturgical movement similar to the C.P.L. of Paris. The initiative came from the Germans. Msgr. Wagner, the director of the Trier Institute, came to participate in the meetings of the C.P.L. with Professor Balthasar Fischer of the Trier School of Theology. More credit is due to Msgr. Wagner because at the beginning he knew French only imperfectly. Father Fischer, on the other hand, spoke it fluently and without an accent. These first contacts began a collaboration which lasted until after Vatican II.

The first international meeting took place in 1951 at Maria

Laach. It was strictly private, that is, it did not include any representatives of the hierarchy and recruited its members by invitation. This was a working group composed of technicians.

Being an expert at international meetings had its advantages: in particular, that of getting to know new places and persons. This time the place was well chosen. Maria Laach, with its lake crowned with wooded hills and its old romanesque church, is a splendid site. As for new persons, the most noteworthy were the monks who accorded us a cordial welcome. I have maintained a friendly relationship with two of them: Dom Odilo Heiming and Dom Burkhard Neunheuser. The latter served as the French-German interpreter. Today he is the director of the Liturgical Institute of Saint Anselm's in Rome. Among those invited, the most well-known was Father Jungmann. He confided to me that when he entered the Society of Jesus, those who knew him were greatly surprised because they expected him to enter the Benedictines at Beuron. He, along with Dom Capelle, was one of the most competent people for the topic under discussion: the Roman Mass.

We experienced the difficulties that come from discussing a reform. It is hard to please everyone and to find objective criteria. Although an agreement was reached on some points, we stumbled over two problems which would still be debated after Vatican II.

The most important was that of the canon of the Roman Mass. The Ordinary of the Mass, such as it was then, had been formed during the Middle Ages—between the ninth and thirteenth centuries by the addition of the celebrant's prayers to a much older nucleus. That is the canon, just as it had been established at the end of the sixth century at the time of Saint Gregory. It is not an inspired text, to be sure, but it has to be treated with special respect. The theologians of the Middle Ages did not try to make it agree with their speculations. They considered it as a given element of tradition and commented on it like a sacred text. One can pass judgment on this exaggerated respect, but what would have happened if the theologians had used the text of the Mass as the jousting field for their quarrels? Could it be imagined that a text, which for thirteen centuries had been at the center of Western Christian piety and which had survived theological controversies unscathed, would finally succumb to a liturgical reform? This didn't concern minor details, like the lists of saints, but a reform of structure. All the critiques would have to be well-founded and the proposed corrections backed up by evidence. But this was far from being the case. The corrections proposed were arbitrary, and they disfigured the text without making up for its real defects.

The second problem, of lesser importance, was that of a penitential rite at the beginning of Mass. The Solemn Mass began with the singing of the Introit while the celebrant and servers recited the *Confiteor* at the foot of the altar. This ceremony did not affect the faithful, and yet the practice of the dialogue Mass had accustomed the people to participate in this confession of sins. Experienced pastors said that people were attached to this practice. It would be useful to envisage a penitential act of the whole congregation, even at solemn Masses. When pastoral experience is invoked I shy away because I'm aware that I have none at all. But I'm not sure that those who speak about it always have much more than I, and yet I take care not to speak up. I had no problem with the introduction of a penitential act. The only difficulty was that we didn't know exactly the place or the form it should take. The problem would not be solved till after Vatican II.

The discussion on the reform of the Mass continued the following year, 1952. The meeting was organized by the Liturgical Commission of Strasbourg which had chosen Mont-Sainte-Odile, the national shrine of Alsace. This is a high, isolated hill on which a basilica was built, along with buildings for accommodating pilgrims and retreatants. But since the location is not easy to reach, we were told to meet in a hotel in Strasbourg where we would be met by car. It was there I made the acquaintance of Msgr. Andrieu. Knowing that Dom Capelle was one of those invited, he had come to meet him. We had time to speak for an hour, but when the cars came to pick us up, Msgr. Andrieu remained in Strasbourg. He was the best historian of the Roman liturgy. His editions of the *Ordines Romani* and the pontificals are admired by all scholars. We would have liked him to come, but a position he had taken was an obstacle: the liturgy could not be reformed; it was a given element of tradition which had to be accepted. He was allergic to the idea that the liturgy could be modified for pastoral goals. The meeting at Mont-Sainte-Odile, like that of Maria Laach, was strictly private. I saw a liturgist who had invited himself jolly well ejected by the organizers. We continued discussing the reforms of the Mass. This time the French-German interpreter was Abbé Rauch, a robust and jovial Alsatian pastor.

In 1953 the meeting was at Lugano; it had a new air about it. I understood then why diplomats like to have their conferences in the Italian-Swiss lake region, and also why they work so poorly. When you're in Lugano in good weather your only wish is to walk along the shores of the lake or sail on it and look at the countryside. But liturgists are more serious people than diplomats. A discussion about the re-edition of ancient liturgical texts was scheduled. I suggested we simply go out, rent a boat, and discuss the question on the lake. A bit of wavering ensued, but finally I had to resign myself to spending that evening inside.

The Lugano meeting was no longer private. More exactly, the sessions of the technicians were paired with a congress open to the public. There were a number of bishops present and even a cardinal, Cardinal Ottaviani. Why he had come, I believe, was a family matter. The organizer of the congress was Father Agustoni, a professor at the Lugano seminary. His brother was the personal secretary of the cardinal, and it was this brother who acted as intermediary to bring the prelate to the congress. Among the bishops present was the bishop of Ghent, Bishop Calewaert. Since we had been fellow students at the University of Louvain, he admitted to me that he was not especially interested in the liturgical movement. But when Cardinal Van Roey wanted a Belgian bishop to be present, he volunteered. He turned out to be hostile to the use of the vernacular, which was being spoken about more and more.

In the public sessions special attention was paid to Holy Week. The reform of the paschal vigil had already been worked out and Father Antonelli, the editor of the provisional rite, was present. But certain critiques had been made and, in all events, the reform of the *Triduum sacrum* still had to be completed.

Parallel to these public sessions there was also a private meeting of experts where the problem of adult baptism was treated. The report was presented by Father Brinkhof, a Dutch Franciscan. Because he showed some reservation about the exorcisms, a little discreet and modest-looking man timidly declared that, in his opinion, the exorcisms were indispensable for mission countries. He was Father Hofinger, former missionary in China and a distinguished missiologist. His contribution was for me a flash of light, and I asked aloud the question that came to my mind: "Are we working for Europe or for the universal church?" The question went beyond the topic of adult baptism. It was somewhat dangerous to think of a liturgical reform with only Europe in mind, especially when pastoral experience was being stressed. This was the first time a missionary took part in our work. I don't know what conclusions the others drew from his intervention. But for me it became evident that a liturgical movement could not be accomplished without wider participation by the missionary world.

In 1954 the tradition of a strictly private technical meeting was readopted. It was held at Mont César. I was in charge of its organization. Two topics were to be treated: the readings of the Mass and concelebration. An unusual event occurred. On the eve of the meeting a letter from the Secretariat of State to a German cardinal, who was not expected, arrived at the abbey. Someone telephoned the nunciature in Brussels to find out if the letter should be forwarded to the addressee or if it were actually destined for the international meeting. Two days later the answer came: the letter was indeed intended for the meeting, and it should be read. So I opened the letter and communicated its text to the group. It was a warning regarding concelebration. We were reminded that we had no competence for making a decision in the matter and that our role was solely to give information. I never received an explanation for this incident. One was suggested to me by a Roman who was familiar with the ways of the Curia. The letter in question was provoked by a denunciation sent from Belgium, probably by a bishop who was upset when he had been informed, incorrectly so, about the aims of the meeting (thus resulting in the mix-up with the German cardinal who had not received an invitation). I know, as a matter of fact, that Dom Capelle had spoken about the meeting to a Belgian bishop who had refused an invitation to attend. I have reason to believe that Dom Capelle, a poor diplomat, had left this bishop with the impression that we wanted to compromise him in a dubious cause, and he had moved first to dissociate himself from the undertaking. I want to stress that it was not Cardinal Van Roey, but I cannot say any more about it.

This is how the problem of concelebration looked at that time. At the meetings or congresses in which many priests took part the question arose of replacing the endless series of private Masses with one Mass at which the priests assisted in alb and stole. The Germans felt that this was a true concelebration and that it was not necessary for all of the priests to pronounce a sacramental formula. I believe that, historically speaking, they were correct. But it was nonetheless evident that Rome would never accept this solution and that, if approval of concelebration was desired, we'd have to lower our expectations and accept a minimal sacramental formula. This was the French position, and it was impossible to get the Germans to agree. A discussion followed which lasted almost the whole night—without results. It was thus impossible to draw up a document which would have had some chance of being approved by Rome. If the Germans had relented, the restoration of concelebration would probably have been attained ten years sooner.

To my knowledge no international meeting was held in 1955. We had to wait till 1956 for another meeting which was called the "First International Congress of Pastoral Liturgy." It was held at Assisi. There, as at Lugano, we had twin sessions: some for experts held before the congress; others open to the public. I attended this private meeting and gave a report on the breviary. Unfortunately, the atmosphere had changed. The authorities were admitted, in particular Cardinal Bea who was the pope's confessor. I took the opportunity to criticize energetically the introduction of new marian feasts and of reading papal encyclicals in the office. I was certain that I was expressing out loud what everyone was thinking, but no one dared follow me up; they let me drop, literally. The presence of Cardinal Bea had tied their tongues. I was furious and swore that I would not be "taken" again. I didn't go to the public sessions. My nephew had come to meet me, and we left for a car trip around Italy. Afterwards I learned that the congress closed in Rome with a discourse of Pius XII in which he condemned silent concelebration. I didn't attend any other international meetings. I was invited to the one which was held at Montserrat, but I refused once again. Other well-known names were to come to that meeting, but I didn't want to repeat the Assisi experience. I knew ahead of time that if I were to say what I thought, no one would have backed me up. Besides, since 1954, I was working on another issue: that of teaching liturgy, something which was much more urgent.

10

Teaching the Liturgy

Summer school courses held at Louvain occupied Dom Botte's attention from 1953 to 1967. These sessions aimed at providing background in liturgy to seminary professors, who generally lacked all specialized training in this field. Paralleling the Louvain courses at this time was a series of summer undergraduate classes at Notre Dame University which invited a number of eminent European liturgical scholars to teach from time to time—among them Louis Bouyer whose *Liturgical Piety* was compiled from a set of lectures given at Notre Dame.

There is a warm human interest flavor to Botte's descriptions of how commemorations were mounted to honor Dom Lambert Beauduin in 1953 on the occasion of his eightieth birthday and again in 1959 on the fiftieth anniversary of the liturgical movement. (Tr.)

I N THE 1950s AND THE FOLLOWING YEARS hopes for a reform of the liturgy and working toward it discreetly were justified. But it was also evident that this reform would be slow in coming and that, at any rate, it was not an alibi for letting other current problems lie dormant. Among these the most urgent was that of teaching. At the beginning of the liturgical movement one of the difficulties was the lack of training for priests. At the turn of the century the seminary liturgy course was purely and simply a course in rubrics. How were things half a century later? The only way to take stock and see whether the young priests were better trained than their older colleagues was to take a survey. The Pastoral Liturgy Center put together a questionnaire which it sent to French-speaking seminaries. We received about fifty responses. The situation differed from diocese to diocese. In some seminaries praiseworthy efforts had been made, but in others the situation had scarcely changed. Just the same, almost all agreed on two points. The first was the limited attention paid by study programs to the liturgy; the second was the professors' lack of training. Most of them complained they were made liturgy professors without warning, without having had the time or the opportunity to gain some degree of competence. Besides, specializing in liturgy was difficult since there was no institute organized for its study. The only way was to do a thesis in theology on a liturgical topic; but most theology schools did not have a chair in liturgy and, consequently, did not have specialized professors. Furthermore, it seemed that superiors didn't dream of giving special preparation to liturgy professors. This was a subject that anyone could teach. Statistics enabled us to note that preference was given to bursars. We can leave to conjecture what the reasons for this preference were, but the facts remain.

On the whole we weren't faced with aged personnel soon due to be replaced. There were some young individuals and men in their prime who still had a whole career ahead of them. What could be done for them?

The Sulpicians were particularly interested because they provided professors for many seminaries. The Studies Committee of Saint-Sulpice, the Pastoral Liturgy Center and the Abbey of Mont César agreed to organize summer courses in Louvain. Why was this city chosen rather than Paris which was certainly more accessible, especially for the French? Because Louvain offered opportunities which couldn't be found in Paris. The seminary in Issy could offer lodging to the participants, but it didn't have a specialized liturgical library which would have allowed study between classes, and it was physically impossible to go to consult the various libraries in Paris. Surely it was important for the liturgy professors to have on hand the documentation which their seminaries lacked. On the other hand, Mont César had the advantage of possessing a well-stocked library. On the tables of the scriptorium could be displayed all the documentation useful for the topics treated, and the participants could go there to work. I remember an old professor who, after twenty years of teaching, opened Lietzmann's edition of the *Gregorian Sacramentary* and said "Oh, so this is what a sacramentary is!" This little incident goes a long way to explain the situation of those professors who never had the indispensable study tools available to them.

These study weeks began in July 1953. The program allowed for sixteen hours of classes spread over six days. This was equivalent to what was expected for schools of theology: one semester with one hour per week. The classes were divided among the various professors. Two of them had four lessons so as to treat thoroughly a special question. The remaining eight hours were given to four other professors. Looking over the list of the programs you can see that most of the courses were given by the same team: Dom Capelle, Canon Chavasse, Canon Martimort, Père Gy, Abbé Jounel, and myself. We were supposed to cover all the material within four years: the Mass, the ritual, the pontifical, the breviary, and the liturgical year. Our intent was not to exhaust the subjects which were treated. Nor was the goal to furnish model courses which the professors could repeat for their own students. These were proficiency courses, designed to introduce those attending to a study of the sources and work methods. The course work could be rounded off by symposia organized on special topics at the participants' request. I don't believe I'm offending my colleagues by saying that the most appreciated courses were those of Canon Chavasse. He was also the most self-sacrificing in responding to questions. I remember that at times I had to rescue him from the interminable symposia which exhausted him. I feel that those who attended these study weeks over a period of several years, and continued to work between the sessions, were able to acquire genuine competence.

I have very good memories of these weeks. Each year I had the joy of welcoming newcomers and the veterans who returned. I was struck by the genuineness of their desire to carry out their mission well: to prepare new priests for the service of Christ and of his church. What brought them to us was not intellectual curiosity, but concern for understanding the meaning of the Christian mystery as it is expressed in the liturgy which is the expression of the faith in prayer. I hope that those who came— the overall list includes 250 names—still have good memories of the time they spent at the abbey in that cordial priestly brotherhood.

Two of these weeks coincided with the celebration of anniversaries. In 1953 Dom Lambert Beauduin reached eighty years of age. I learned that a French Dominican, Père Pie Duployé, who belonged to the C.P.L., intended to publish some old articles of Dom Beauduin in a collection that would be called *Ossa humiliata.* This title was justified by the fact that authors published in this collection had difficulties with the Holy See at one time or other. The idea of publishing the articles of Dom Beauduin for his eightieth birthday seemed excellent, but it seemed untimely to do it with an eye-catching title that recalled hard times. Besides, if a tribute were to be paid to Dom Beauduin, it would have been quite odd for it to be tendered by a foreigner and not by his confreres. With the consent of the prior of Chevetogne I wrote a friendly letter to Père Duployé asking him to join us in offering a volume of *Miscellanea* to the jubilarian. I received a curt and haughty refusal which cut short any discussion. I then informed Père Duployé that Chevetogne and Mont César would take care of editing the *Miscellanea.* I believe that the collection *Ossa humiliata* was never published.

I myself prepared the set of articles for the *Miscellanea,* which was printed in 1953. Dom Beauduin arrived from Chevetogne for an afternoon session. Upon entering he received warm applause. I invited him to go up to the speaker's table from where he gave a short talk to the group. Then I gave him a copy of the *Miscellanea* with a Latin dedication which I read aloud. The session ended with a lecture by Canon Chavasse. At the end there occurred a humorous incident due to the absent-mindedness of Dom Capelle. During Canon Chavasse's lecture Dom Lambert was seated in front of the first table next to Dom Capelle. Dom Beauduin placed on the table the volume that had been presented to him. When it was time to leave, Dom Capelle put the book under his arm and moved toward the door. He had to be detained and was informed that he too would receive a copy, but this one was intended for Dom Lambert.

In 1959 we began the fiftieth anniversary of the liturgical movement. Cardinal Van Roey agreed to preside at an academic convocation during the July session. Since Dom Beauduin's health was increasingly delicate, this seemed to be the last chance for obtaining from the pope a word of thanks and encouragement for

Dom Beauduin's devoted service to the church. I asked Cardinal Van Roey to take the necessary steps. He asked his representative in Rome, Msgr. Joliet, to handle the matter. The latter went to the Secretariat of State and was received by Msgr. Veuillot, then in charge of the Secretariat's French correspondence, who asked Msgr. Joliet for a written document. Msgr. Joliet in turn wrote to Malines to ask for a letter, but Cardinal Van Roey became angry. His secretary, Msgr. Leclef, sent me a letter which said that the Cardinal's reply was: "They should know in Rome that Msgr. Joliet is my representative; I won't write any letter." The Cardinal was probably right, but this was of no help to us. Was a stupid question of protocol to deprive an old dying man like Dom Lambert of his final consolation? I knew I had no chance of getting the Cardinal to change his mind, so I sent the letter from his secretary to Dom Benoît Becker, procurator of the Belgian Benedictine Congregation in Rome. He went to the Secretariat of State and persuaded Msgr. Veuillot to accept Msgr. Leclef's letter as the missing written document. The letter of John XXIII arrived on time.

Unfortunately, Dom Beauduin's health had worsened and bringing him to Louvain was out of the question. Dom Rousseau had Dom Lambert record a brief spoken message which was played during the academic convocation. I read the letter from John XXIII, recalled the origins of the liturgical movement, and paid tribute to two veterans of the movement who were present. One was Dom Franco de Wyels of the Affligem Abbey who was among the very first colleagues of Dom Beauduin for the Flemish part of the country. After World War I he followed Dom Lambert in his ecumenical undertaking, and then he returned to his abbey where he was elected abbot. The monastery of Affligem had become the center of the Dutch-speaking liturgical movement. The second veteran was Dom Gaspar Lefebvre. His name was so well-known for so long in France that it became identified with a missal and no longer just an author's name: you bought a "Dom Lefebvre." Still, he was there, quite alive, even though he had passed his eightieth birthday.

Wednesday afternoons during the study weeks were free, and we usually organized excursions for those who wanted them. That year I succeeded in requisitioning enough cars to send everybody off to Chevetogne. Thus all were able to greet, for one last time, the man who had been the originator of the liturgical movement.

The study weeks continued till 1967. Except for the one in 1963, all were held at Mont César. During the last years I handed over their management to a younger confrere, Dom François Vandenbroucke, who had become director of *Questions liturgiques et paroissiales.*

In 1963 the Studies Committee of Saint-Sulpice asked me to hold that year's study week at Issy-les-Moulineaux with pedagogical questions as the theme. They also asked me to give a talk. I don't think it was ever published, even though I left the text with the editors of the *Bulletin de Saint-Sulpice.* I broadened the subject matter a bit and pointed out two defects that threatened seminary teaching. The first was a lack of cohesiveness in the faculty. Specialists in different fields had been trained, and each one did his best in his own domain but without any concern for what others were doing in their areas. The students, torn between the different approaches, couldn't reach a synthesis for themselves. The second defect was the overly passive character of teaching. To listen to the professor and give correct answers during the exams was all right, but not enough. The priest must be able to continue his training. But many are incapable of this because they were never taught to work on their own. The remedy is for professors to act as a team and to agree on how to have the students work according to individual abilities. I know this is possible because I've experienced it. Without a doubt a seminary is not a university, but it's surprising what an average student can do with help and encouragement. You don't ask for original writings that deserve publication but, for example, an explanation of a problem, a book report, a critique of an article—it doesn't matter which, as long as it requires personal effort from the student. Unfortunately, I've been forced to recognize that rarely were there seminaries where this was the direction followed. I will return to this topic in connection with the Institut Supérieur de Liturgie. I added in the talk a few personal reflections about teaching. I never took any courses in pedagogy, and it's possible that my ideas on the subject are not orthodox. They've come to me by experience as a student and as a professor. I took courses until I was thirty, and I've been a professor for forty years in higher and university level education. I had all the time needed to realize there are good teachers and there are bad teachers, and that the distance between them lies not always in the order of learning but in that of psychology. Obviously a professor has to master the material taught and not be a slave to a book or to written notes. But this is not enough. I had a confrere who was an excellent theologian and who carefully prepared his classes. Still, he bored his students to death. What he said went over their heads. And to top it all off, he had a strange delivery. He spoke, if you could call it that, in spurts; the flow gave the annoying impression of machine gun fire. As I was on excellent terms with him, I ventured one day to ask him whether he sometimes got the impression he bored his students. His candid answer was that he had never noticed anything. A person, no matter how learned, who has no contact with the audience will never be a good professor. The first principle of a teacher is never to be boring. You might ask whether I have ever bored my students. Of course I have! But I would notice this after ten minutes, and I would tell myself that I was at fault and that I had to try to stir up attention in one way or another. The second principle is that you must answer the students' questions. I've always allowed myself to be interrupted by requests for explanations. When I didn't have an answer right away, I left it for later on, rather than bluffing and answering just anything. Students know how to appreciate intellectual honesty.

These study weeks responded to a temporary situation. We had to provide liturgy professors with an opportunity of acquiring the training no one ever dreamed of giving them. But it was necessary to foresee a changing of the guard in a few years, and we didn't want to turn an improvised solution into a system. We had to find a way of training professors before their appointment. A student wanting to do this was very much at a loss. No institute provided special preparation for liturgists. As a result, we had to create something entirely new.

11

The Paris Institut Supérieur de Liturgie

The year 1956 saw the establishment of a graduate institute of liturgical studies at the Institut Catholique of Paris. Dom Botte served as its first director and here describes in detail its approach to the teaching of liturgy. Many present-day liturgy scholars, teachers, and other professionals received their training at the institute. Negotiations for Rome's approval of the school as a pontifical institute and the ironing out of some difficulties with the Paris Pastoral Liturgy Center show Botte's acumen for unavoidable political interventions. (Tr.)

AN ARTICLE IN THE NEWSPAPER *La Croix* in 1956 announced the forthcoming establishment of a liturgical institute attached to the School of Theology of the Institut Catholique of Paris, under the direction of the C.P.L. and the Abbey of Mont César. The person most surprised by this news was Dom Capelle, the abbot of Mont César: he didn't recall having given his consent. Was this a lapse of memory on his part, or was it rather that he had not been consulted? I was never able to discover the answer to this question with certitude, but the establishment of an institute seemed necessary to me. I persuaded Dom Capelle to agree. He gave me his approval and the task of negotiating with the C.P.L.

The two main points to be determined were the specific aims of the institute and its program. Teaching can occur on different levels: engineers and simple technicians are not trained in the same school. One could have imagined a liturgical institute open to a very wide public, just like the Institut Catéchétique attended by many teaching sisters. But if we wanted to prepare seminary professors of liturgy, then the level had to be different. On this point there was full agreement. We had to provide a steady supply of seminary professors.

The question of the program was next. I sent a long and detailed draft which covered everything to be said about liturgy. It was very well thought-out, but it was more the outline of an encyclopedia than a program of advanced studies. The projected courses were so numerous and so diverse that I could not see who would be able to teach all of them with competence. All kinds of topics would be touched upon without any of them being treated in-depth. Moreover, there was no opportunity assigned for the personal work of the students. I drew up a counter-draft which I submitted to the C.P.L., and this was accepted as the basis of discussion. Next I had a long talk with Père Gy and Père Louis Bouyer in Paris. The latter was very helpful to us because he was a professor at the Institut Catholique and knew all its resources. We would be able to rely upon existing courses in the different schools to fill out our program (from Theology, Canon Law, and Letters), or we could turn to the various institutes connected with the Institut Catholique like the Institut Catéchétique or the Institut Grégorien. We had, then, set up a concrete program. The next morning we went to see Msgr. Blanchet, rector of the Institut Catholique. Canon Martimort, who had just arrived from Toulouse, joined us for the meeting. The draft was adopted without any difficulty.

Next to be chosen were a director and the faculty. For director I suggested Père Bouyer who was a resident of Paris, but he did not accept and insisted that I take the position. I did not hesitate in accepting because I didn't see anyone else in particular who was available. Dom Capelle was more competent than I, but it was impossible for him to effectively direct an institute—this would have been no more than a juridical fiction. Canon Martimort would have made an excellent director, but family reasons prevented him from leaving Toulouse. Furthermore, he was already in charge of the C.P.L., something which kept him quite busy. Père

Gy at this time was too young to take upon himself the responsibilities of this position, but he was chosen as assistant-director.
Abbé Jounel was made secretary, and Père Dalmais was made a
professor. The four of us made up the central team of the Institute.
Other professors had been lined up, but an understanding of their
role would come from determining the nature of the program.

To establish it I was guided by the principle that the essential
thing in a liturgy course is to give a commentary on the texts
which constitute an important part of the church's tradition. But to
be able to give such a commentary with authority two things are
indispensable: a knowledge of liturgical sources and a critical
work method. It was toward this personal training that we had to
give an orientation to the Institute. So we weren't going to provide
for the future teachers some sample courses which they could
later on provide for their students; instead, we would enable them
to prepare the courses themselves. To attain this goal the program
would include four elements: a number of general courses, special courses, some electives, and seminars.

The general courses were of an introductory nature. They included a general introduction given in the first semester and a
double cycle spread out over two years. The general introduction
was heavily bibliographical: it acquainted the students with the
principal work tools they would have to use. The other two
courses concerned the history of the liturgy. One covered the eras
of general liturgical history; the other treated in a more particular
way the Roman liturgy by studying the formation of the different
compilations as the missal, pontifical, ritual, and breviary. These
sources provided an overall view of the liturgy and the questions
it raises, but they were not enough to give the students a personal
formation. To teach them how to work they needed another kind
of course, namely, the special course.

There's no better way of teaching someone than by having this
person watch an expert at work and then attempt to imitate the expert. This is just as true in the realm of learning as it is in cooking.
Every graduate institution should have some in-depth courses
where the professor is not limited to pronouncing authoritative
statements, but goes on to show how the professor's technique
operates and justifies the conclusions which are reached. What
was special about our Institute was the way we did not limit these
courses to only one professor, but called upon a team of the best
specialists we could find. There were five series of special courses

each semester. Each professor gave six lectures spread over two weeks. This was enough time to treat a specific problem in-depth and to give the students an example of methodology. The courses were given by Dom Capelle; Professors Chavasse, Vogel, and Munier of Strasbourg; Professor Fischer from Trier; Père de Gaiffier the Bollandist; Canon Martimort; Père Bouyer; and Père Chenu. Our students had the unhoped-for opportunity of meeting with such authorities and of benefiting from their experience.

The electives, which the students themselves could choose, covered subjects which were related to the liturgy. At the beginning of the semester each student was to choose two courses offered in the general catalogue of the Institut Catholique. Thus, those who wanted to study the oriental rites found courses in ancient languages at the Institut Oriental. The Faculté de Lettres had courses in Christian Latin and in paleography. The Institut Grégorien had a course in musical paleography. The Institut Catéchétique offered a course on the history of catechetics and a course on pastoral liturgy. The reason we did not include a pastoral course among our general courses was to avoid duplicating the one Père Roguet was already giving at the Institut Catéchétique.

All the same, these theoretical courses called for a complement. Learning how to work involves seeing what a competent specialist does, but it also requires that the student try to imitate the specialist. The special courses provided examples of methodology. And yet the students still had to try to apply the theoretical principles and learn how to conduct scholarly research on their own. As a result, we placed essential importance on the seminars. These appeared to take up only a small part of the program—one hour a week. Yet each session required several hours of preparation from the students. A group of them met under the direction of a professor to study a special topic. The professor was on hand only to assign work projects and correct mistakes, whereas the work was done by the students. The weekly session helped verify the progress of their research and to evaluate the methodology, but the work as such took place outside of class hours and required a good part of the students' time. Along with the liturgy seminars there was a seminar on canon law directed by a layman, Professor Gaudemet, who taught at the Université de Paris and at Strasbourg's Institut de Droit Canonique.

The only change which the program underwent concerned

Latin. At the beginning we sent all the students to the courses of Christian Latin given at the Faculté de Lettres. These courses were excellent, but after a few years I realized that they weren't adapted to the majority of our students who weren't philologists and whose background was too elementary. The courses at the Faculté de Lettres still remained electives, but I added—for the first year students—a course of Latin applied to the liturgical texts.

The orientation of the Institute was evident. Its purpose was not to give the students an encyclopedic knowledge of the liturgy, based on an extensive number of university lectures. These lectures were reduced to a minimum in favor of the personal training and work of the students.

At the beginning the Institute had to face some difficulties. The first concerned the recruiting of students. The Institute was established as a service to French seminaries. But the French bishops sent almost no students to us. Fortunately, students came from foreign countries: from Spain, Italy, Holland, Belgium, and even from North and South America. The Institute will always remain very international, and we had in our classes representatives of twenty different nationalities.

The second difficulty was the deficient training of certain students. Nonetheless, we stipulated that the candidates had to possess a degree on a par with the licentiate in theology. In reality, however, several had not earned the licentiate, and we even had to admit that this degree did not always mean that much. It seems that in certain schools the licentiate is a type of bachelor's degree rather than proof of a serious course of studies.

Previously I alluded to the deficient traning of those who had gone to the seminary. This can be seen by their ignorance of Latin—even on the part of those who had taken courses in the humanities. It seems that their theological studies led them to forget what they have learned in college. After a while we had the candidates take an entrance examination in Latin, and we were forced to exclude many who really knew nothing at all. As far as the others were concerned, the average level of competency wasn't very high—about fourth year Latin. This is why I decided to give a course of more basic Latin than that taught at the Faculté de Lettres. Nevertheless, this course appeared very difficult to some of the students. Actually, it was no more than high school Latin. I know what I'm talking about since I taught high school for twelve years and know what you can get out of students aged fifteen to eighteen. I explained the liturgical texts in the same way I used to do for the classical Latin texts, and I took the opportunity to review syntax. Still, it was difficult to obtain from the students an exact analysis of a form and the reason for its use.

Another deficiency was the lack of a critical sense. At one of our seminars a student was supposed to explain a canon from a council in Gaul. He gave me the French translation found in Dom Leclercq's history of the councils. When I asked the student to give me the exact details, he became quite upset: he had just discovered that the Christians in Gaul did not speak French. But then where would he find the Latin text? He didn't seem to know that Mansi or the other collections of the councils existed. Next he cited a Greek Father in Migne's Latin version. I asked him what were the words of the original? He was completely lost. He hadn't even dreamed of taking a quick look at the Greek in the parallel column.

This lack of a critical sense was seen in the special courses. The students were ready to accept every authoritative statement. They acknowledged the competence of their professors, but when we tried to show them what methodology enabled us to come to our conclusions, they were no longer interested. This wasn't practical enough. The courses of Dom Capelle and Canon Chavasse weren't the kind the students expected to give to a class of seminarians, so it was enough to retain their conclusions—the rest had no real use. Some even wished that these special courses be discontinued. It was out of the question that we should deprive good students of this advanced training in order to suit the tastes of a few slouches; but the presence of the latter created a dead weight which we would have to remove if we were to keep the Institute on a university level.

We had a student who, after returning to his own country, spread the story that the courses at the Institute were so difficult that even a doctor of theology could not pass them. I feel I ought to put things into their proper perspective. We had a student with a doctorate in theology from Ottawa. He took our program for two years and used to tell over and over again—to whomever was interested in hearing it—that all these courses weren't practical enough. Nevertheless, he wanted to obtain an advanced diploma which involved the writing of a thesis. But in order to be allowed to present the thesis, one had to take a special examination designed to check the student's study skills and not a wide range of facts. He came one morning to the library of the C.P.L. and selected one of the several topics that were proposed to him. He was supposed to work on it for a whole day by using the library. We didn't ask from him a complete study or one that was very well written up. We wanted to see how he was able to handle the work; whether he was capable of putting together a bibliography, and whether he knew how to find the sources and interpret them correctly. He chose to work on the Christmas cycle of the Roman Rite from the fourth to the eighth century, and he treated the topic without consulting any of the sources of this rite, be they the sacramentary, lectionary, or the antiphonary. This was really quite a feat. He relied on some data derived from second- or third-hand articles, but he was unable to manage the sources well. We concluded that he wasn't adequately trained to be allowed to present a scholarly thesis. Yet I can attest to the fact that many students who didn't have a doctorate from Ottawa passed this infamous exam without difficulty because they had learned to work competently rather than just being satisfied with what they thought was practical.

After our first few years in operation, I thought of asking for Rome's approval of the Institute. This was not inspired by ultramontaine preoccupations, but for a practical reason. The Institute was the first and the only one of its kind, but I was more or less sure that a similar one would not be long in coming on the Roman scene itself. Even though this would be quite natural, there was a danger that once a Pontifical Institute of Liturgy had been established, we would be isolated and ignored. This is what happened with the Biblical Institute. Thanks to Père Lagrange, a school of biblical studies was founded in Jerusalem, but the privileges and favors were reserved for the Biblical Institute at Rome which alone was empowered to grant academic degrees. The same thing could quite possibly happen to us if we did not succeed in having ourselves recognized before a Roman institute was established. During a meeting of our board of directors I proposed to move in this direction. Msgr. Blanchet remarked that he agreed, but that he did not know how to proceed. This struck me as being quite strange for a rector of a Catholic university, but I told him that I knew what steps should be taken. I presented him with the text of a request which he would sign and then have countersigned by the local ordinary. I would then take care of the other formalities.

This first step did not, to my knowledge, bring about any response. Only later on did I suspect that Msgr. Blanchet received a negative reply which he did not pass on to me so as to let the whole thing drop. This did not help matters. There was a sure means of receiving an answer: our request would be handled, no longer by the rector, but by the Cardinal Archbishop of Paris and be addressed to Cardinal Pizzardo, the prefect of the Congregation of Seminaries and Universities. One cardinal is obliged to answer another cardinal. Msgr. Blanchet was most unwilling in this regard, and I was able to obtain my document only by directly approaching the archdiocesan chancery. Cardinal Pizzardo's answer was negative: it said that after consultation with competent authorities in the field of liturgy he could not grant his approval because of some abuses and errors in this field.

The authorities in the field of liturgy were obviously the Congregation of Rites. I sent another letter to Cardinal Cicognani, the prefect of the Congregation of Rites, asserting that the Institute had nothing to do with errors and abuses in liturgy; that it was an Institute of advanced training, established for the purpose of acquainting future professors with the authentic tradition of the church; and that if he wished to find out about the spirit of the Institute he could check with one of his close collaborators, Father Antonelli, who had sent us one of his young confreres, Father Falsini (an Italian Franciscan), to take courses in Paris. I also wrote to Cardinal Pizzardo and pointed out that attention seemingly had not been paid to the documentation that had been sent to him, that is, the statutes of the Institute and the list of courses.

I received no answer from Cardinal Cicognani, and this did not surprise me. What did surprise me, on the other hand, was Cardinal Pizzardo's reply. He frankly admitted that they had mistaken the Institute for the Paris Pastoral Liturgy Center. An examination of the documentation resulted in a correction of the error and, as a result, approval would be possible after a couple of years on a trial basis. The cardinal asked me, in the meantime, to watch out that the Institute remain within the limits established by the statutes, and he made it clear that there were to be no practical applications, not even applied theory.

To me, this letter contained both good and bad news. The bad news was that the C.P.L. was poorly regarded in Rome and that people there considered it responsible for the anarchy which was beginning to spread. This was unfair, as I wrote to the cardinal.

But it was a fact that I couldn't really do anything about it. Happily, the letter also contained some good news. The approval of the Institute seemed no longer just possible, but probable. I had some accompanying information through Dom Benôit Becker whom I asked to represent me in Rome. He was in contact with Msgr. Romeo, the consultor who was given the job of looking after this question by Cardinal Pizzardo. The monsignor was very favorable toward my position, but he feared the influence of the C.P.L. Several members of the C.P.L. had been to Rome where they had spoken of "their" Institute, and this was the source of the mix-up which occurred in the Congregation of Rites (to which my file had not been referred). The Congregation of Seminaries retained the file, and Msgr. Romeo was able to look into it. He approved it, but wondered whether the influence of the C.P.L. might give the Institute another orientation. Hence, the injunctions imposed upon me by the cardinal's letter. I was also asked for a letter of recommendation from the dean of the School of Theology to which we were attached. I approached Père Leclerc, dean at that time, who was very well disposed toward us. He acted imprudently because he spoke about it to the rector, Msgr. Blanchet, who forbade him to send out anything at all—Rome had refused, we were not supposed to do anything else. It was at this point that I noticed that the feelings of Msgr. Blanchet had been ambiguous from the very beginning. He had given his theoretical agreement, but he had to be pressed about the smallest steps to be taken. He did not want to see this approval and regretted having been connected with it. So he was happy over Rome's refusal and wanted to bury the whole question. I didn't insist—the cause was well underway. It was enough to carry on just as we had begun and wait for another opportunity.

At this very time the C.P.L. undertook an untimely initiative. It decided to organize a series of courses on pastoral liturgy at its center in Neuilly. It had the right to do so, and I had no reason to find fault with them, provided the Institute would not be involved in the program. But our students were invited: they received an invitation to these classes along with the program of the Institute. No one asked my opinion, and I was not even informed. There was at least a lack of courtesy here, but I would not have taken so much offense from this if the initiative had not placed me in an impossible position vis-à-vis Rome. A few days after receiving the Congregation's instructions we were sending our students to take pastoral courses at C.P.L. This would appear as a rather gross stratagem for getting around Rome's directives, exactly the type of mistake we should not have made since it would confirm the fears of the Congregation. As soon as I was alerted, I wrote to Père Roguet and asked him to postpone this plan for pastoral courses. I was counting on a quick answer because the opening of the academic year was upon us, and I had to state my position from the very first day. Père Roguet's response never arrived due to a mistake in the address; as a result, I had to exercise my responsibility before giving the first class.

I went about this in as friendly a way as I was able: I told the students that the pastoral courses at Neuilly represented something entirely normal among the activities of the C.P.L., but these courses were not designed for the students of the Institute. The C.P.L. courses were aimed at French priests in the active ministry and sought solutions to problems of the church in France. These solutions, though very legitimate in themselves, could not be applied to all the situations around the world. The Institute was of an international make-up, and it did not have as its goal the formation of ready-made solutions for resolving problems everywhere, but to train the students so that they would be able to find solutions once they had returned to their own countries. Moreover, I had received definite instructions from Rome to the effect that the Institute should keep its scholarly orientation and not become active in the practical domain. In order to avoid any misunderstanding I asked the students not to attend any of the pastoral courses. After telling them this, I began my class.

I thought the incident was closed, but I was wrong. A few days later, after my return to Louvain, I received a telephone call from Paris. I was told that there had been an agitated meeting at the C.P.L. and that a messenger was being dispatched by plane to come see me. I immediately left to meet him at Zaventem, the Brussels airport, and I took him into Brussels where he brought me up to date on the situation. That morning there had been a meeting of the C.P.L. staff in Paris, and everyone was upset with my intervention. This proved to me that the pastoral courses had been intended for our students and that the plan was to present me with a fait accompli, because there was nothing to prevent the C.P.L. from having its pastoral courses for other groups of people. But my action had established a question of principle. This could have been resolved in five minutes' time if they had only decided to look at the statutes of the Institute, but no one had thought of doing so. They closed ranks against me, and the messenger was given the task of informing me of the position of the C.P.L. He described it at length and with conviction. The Institute was founded by the C.P.L. Mont César was associated with the Institute as a gesture of friendship, but this did not modify the basic state of affairs. The Institute remained the property of the C.P.L. and was controlled by it. I was only delegated by the C.P.L. and was accountable to its directors. This was really a bit crude, and I didn't know whether the person I was speaking with himself believed what he was saying. I listened calmly to this description without giving my own point of view. The idea of settling the question between planes when there wasn't any urgent deadline seemed childish to me. I took the messenger back to his return flight and left him with the impression that he had fulfilled his mission well and that he had brought me around to reason. One must never cross people without necessity.

I waited a few weeks before settling the question. Time was needed to let feelings calm down. It was out of the question that I should appear before a full meeting of the C.P.L. which had no competence to judge me. I wanted to let them know in a friendly way my position through the good services of a very respected member of the C.P.L., Père Louvel, who was then director of *Fêtes et Saisons*. One day I invited him to have lunch at the Thoumieux restaurant where I explained to him my point of view on condition that he would then relate it to the others.

I didn't make this move without taking some precautions. From the first year on I formulated some statutes which had been accepted by all the signers and which, at that moment, were being considered for approval by the Holy See. These were the only possible basis for a juridical discussion. According to this document the C.P.L. and the Abbey of Mont César were co-founders of the Institut Supérieur de Liturgie. Both had the right of nominating a candidate for the director's position, but the rector of the Institut Catholique had the right to choose the director. The Institut Supérieur de Liturgie was run by a board of directors which had seven members: the rector, the dean of the School of Theology, the director, the assistant director, the secretary of the Institute, a delegate of the C.P.L., and a delegate of Mont César. The C.P.L., then, had one vote out of seven. This was printed black on white, and one didn't have to be an expert to see I was not at all a subordinate of the directors of the C.P.L. I was accountable only to the rector and the board of directors. The day-to-day running of the Institute was my responsibility; for more important questions I asked the opinion of the board. Sending our students to take pastoral courses was a very serious question, and I would not have assumed responsibility for this on my own. If I had been told about this in advance, I would have submitted the question to the board of directors, and the proposal would have been rejected by the majority of them. I could not give in to a decision taken against the rules. Besides, in this specific case I would not have been able to accept a favorable decision by the board: Cardinal Pizzardo has just made me responsible for the functioning of the Institute and had given me precise instructions. I would then have been obliged to present the case to Rome, something which would have amounted to suicide for us.

Père Louvel perfectly understood the problem. He also understood the reasons for my opposition to the establishment of pastoral courses. Like myself, he saw that we shouldn't mix the two levels of teaching. The alternative was established from the beginning, and all agreed that we would give university-style training. If I had been given the position as director, it was, I believe, for the reason that my name was a guarantee of the teaching level. I couldn't let just anything happen under my name—it was a question of being upright about the matter. I couldn't let the Institute go downhill from an advanced level to a level of practical techniques. I laid my cards on the table from the very beginning. I had deceived no one, but I know from experience that it is difficult to keep the training at a definite level. The precautions that I took turned out to be effective.

After this meeting with Père Louvel I considered the incident closed, and it was in fact. It's the only conflict I had with the C.P.L., and it didn't leave any trace afterwards. As far as I'm concerned, I never made a tragedy out of the affair, and my friends at the C.P.L. did not insist on it either. I have every reason to believe that they—thinking back on it—recognized that my position was well-founded.

The question of approval soon came up in a rather urgent way. The establishment of a Pontifical Institute of Liturgy was announced for the immediate future at the College of Saint Anselm under the direction of the Benedictines. It was either now or never for us to make our move. I made several personal interventions.

Several well-informed persons like Father Antonelli and Father Bugnini were at the Congregation of Rites, and they understood that refusing to approve us while approving the new institute would amount to an injustice and a scandal—and they knew that I would not hesitate to make this known. The scandal involved would have been all the greater since one of the main organizers of the Roman institute had been trained at ours. Dom Adrien Nocent was the first of our students to receive the advanced degree. Would they be able to appoint him a professor of a Roman institute and at the same time refuse to recognize our degrees? I also tried to have Monsieur de Margerie, the ambassador of France to the Holy See, intervene. At the Congregation of Seminaries I was persona grata with Msgr. Romeo. Nevertheless, I asked Msgr. Cerfaux, who knew him well, to stir up his zeal. Regardless of the means taken, the decree of approval arrived. Our institute was saved; it was on an equal footing with the Roman institute. Of course there would be competition, but this would be honest competition based on the quality of training and not on privileges. In this realm we would be able to keep up.

There was, however, a shadow on the wall. The dislike of the Congregation —or Congregations—for the C.P.L. had not abated. The name of the C.P.L. had been obliterated from the brief historical sketch which began the decree of approval. I say "obliterated" and not "omitted" because the document which I had submitted mentioned the C.P.L. at the very beginning. This could not have been an accidental omission. The establishment of the Institute was attributed to several Benedictines. This was as stupid as it was unjust, but I could not change it at all. I did the only thing possible: I placed the official document in the archives of the Institute; I let people know its contents; but I never had the full text published.

In 1963 I reached seventy and, according to the by-laws of the Institut Catholique, I was supposed to be replaced as director. But, for one reason or the other, my term was prolonged for a year. The following year I was replaced by Père Gy. Still, I remained a professor at the Institute till 1969.

I must pay homage to my main collaborators: Père Gy, Abbé Jounel, Père Dalmais: we came to form a perfectly unified team, and I believe we were able to work well together. We were assisted by eminent liturgists who accepted doing special courses for us. If we had in the student body some individuals who caused problems, I think that the majority are thankful to us for the training they received. They are scattered pretty much around the world, but many remain in contact with their former professors. I've been host to more than one who came to Mont César, and still do, as they prepare their theses. My only regret is that we did not have more candidates from mission countries. Unless I be mistaken, the only African we had was Abbé Gervais Mutembe from Rwanda. He did very well, and today is doing good work in his country. We had some future missionaries, some of whom were very interested in the Eastern rites which opened to them perspectives helpful for adaptation in mission countries.

The Institute has carried on under the direction of Père Gy. Vatican II has changed many things, but I believe that a knowledge of the liturgical tradition of the West and the East will always be necessary if the liturgical movement is not to fall into anarchy. But that is another problem.

12

The Saint-Serge Weeks

The long and rich relationship of Botte with Orthodox
Christians, which began in the early 1950s, is highlighted in
this short chapter. Located a little east of Montmartre in Paris,
the Saint-Serge theological center brings together ecumenical groups to study liturgical tradition every year (the translator still receives a yearly personal invitation to attend these
sessions during the summer).

Botte teamed up with Bishop Cassien of Saint-Serge to edit
collections of papers given during the weeks. Two of the
more frequently cited volumes prepared by them concern
the Liturgy of the Hours (*La prière des heures*, 1963) and the
Christmas-Epiphany cycle (*Nöel, Épiphanie, retour du Christ*,
1967). As in several other ways, Botte proved himself a
pioneer by promoting ecumenical study of the liturgy long
before such endeavors were accepted by Rome. (Tr.)

I N 1952 I RECEIVED A LETTER from a person whose name was unfamiliar to me: Père Cyprian Kern of the Russian Orthodox
Institute in Paris. He had learned—I don't know how—that I
was due to go to Paris, and he wanted to discuss with me a project
of his, a project he had already spoken about to Dom Beauduin.
The latter had advised him to approach me. This is why, one day, I
set out to find 93 rue de Crimée in the nineteenth arrondissement,

a neighborhood completely unfamiliar to me. Naturally, I entered the street at the wrong end, that is, the upper end, and had to walk down an endless slope before stopping at number 93. I was standing in front of a rather narrow iron gate. Once I had passed through it, I climbed a concrete ramp which led to a kind of green oasis where a few houses surrounded a rustic chapel. Since there were no signs, I picked a house at random and rang the bell. It was the right one. Père Kern was summoned: he was a man of tall stature, thin, and his eastern monk's habit rendered him even more stately. He had clear eyes, a deep voice. He greeted me most cordially, led me up to his room, and personally prepared for me a cup of Turkish coffee. Then began a long conversation.

He explained the Institut Saint-Serge to me. After the defeat of the White Army, the Russian emigrés flocked to France, especially the Paris region. They had to get organized, not only materially but also spiritually. Among the emigrés were some Orthodox priests who would be able to tend adequately to their spiritual needs for a while; but the future had to be provided for and organized since hopes of returning to Russia were remote. Their dream, then, was to create a school of theology to prepare future priests. Professors and candidates were on hand but a building was needed, and a community of immigrants does not possess vast resources. Still, an opportunity presented itself. In the nineteenth arrondissement there was a German Lutheran foundation which, in virtue of the Treaty of Versailles, had been seized as German property and had to be put up for sale. Thanks to the intervention of a kind Jew whose portrait still hangs in the refectory, the Orthodox community was able to purchase it. The Institut Saint-Serge took up quarters in this foundation. The Lutheran chapel was changed into an Orthodox church. D. Steletzky, a Russian artist, painted the apse and iconostasis. For over thirty years the Institute was able to train a good many priests and had become a religious and intellectual center international in character. Students were now arriving from Greece and other eastern countries. The Russians had not entrenched themselves in their domain as in a fortress. They had established cordial relations with the Catholic world around them. As a result, they were invited to ecumenical meetings. And this is where the plans of Père Kern came in.

At first Père Kern attended these meetings between Catholics and Protestants, but he became more and more ill-at-ease. As he told me, he sometimes avoided them. The first reason was that the talk centered about burning issues for which agreements were never found. The impression was one of going around in circles. Furthermore, the speakers at these meetings were primarily Catholics and Protestants, that is, Westerners discussing Western problems among themselves. Père Kern didn't see what he, the representative of a small emigré community, could contribute to these controversies. Then an idea occurred to him: what if things could be considered the other way around. Instead of discussing what separates us, why not talk about what brings us closer together? Wouldn't we move ahead, if not more quickly at least more surely? He believed that liturgy would be an ideal area for such encounters. Every person would study one's own tradition in a positive fashion, without polemical preoccupations. In this way we would arrive at knowing and understanding each other better. This return to the sources would benefit everyone. There was no question of deriving conclusions or of expressing one's wishes. Spectacular or immediate results should not be expected. Still, this would be a new way of approaching the problem, by relying on convergences more than on differences. Père Kern had spoken about this to Dom Beauduin who warmly encouraged him. Thus it was that the founder of the liturgical movement in 1909 and one who, after World War II, had contributed toward the establishment of the C.P.L., found himself involved in the beginnings of a new initiative.

Just recently I asked myself about this idea of Père Kern: did it come to him naturally without any outside influence, or was it suggested to him—maybe without his even knowing it—by a similar undertaking? I don't have any definite answer to this question. And it certainly does not take any credit away from Père Kern. While I was putting my recollections together, I was struck by a coincidence in dates. In 1951 the first Patristic Congress organized by Professor Cross was held in Oxford. Since patristics is a science, the idea of a congress on the subject was not original to the English. However, it is not a science like others. Those concerned with it are generally members of various Christian confessions and, in all events, are interested in religious problems. Likewise, those who shared in organizing the congress knew that Professor Cross insisted that it be interconfessional. With a knapsack on his back he traveled all over Europe to invite Catholics and Protestants. Those who were personal acquaintances of Professor Cross knew he was in favor of the church's unity. In his appartment there was a large portrait of Pius XII. There can be no doubt that his deep desire was, on the basis of the patristic tradition, to further reconciliation between the different Christian confessions. It seems indisputable to me that Père Kern's intention was closely akin to that of Professor Cross. Was he aware of it? I'm not sure, because the ecumenical facet of the Patristic Congress was less evident than its scholarly side. The parallel is not any less striking. In September 1951 the first Patristic Congress was held at Oxford. In 1952 Père Kern drew up plans for a Study Week at Saint-Serge. At the end of June 1953 the first Week opened. Professor Cross was invited and gave a talk. Thus Père Kern had been corresponding with him, and it is difficult to see in this a mere coincidence. I am inclined to believe that Père Kern had grasped the deep intent of the professor from Oxford and that ecumenism must rely upon—before all else—a dispassionate study of tradition. Père Kern's distinctive merit lies in his application of the same principle to the liturgy.

The first Oxford Congress presented a problem for some Catholics. Would participation in an interconfessional meeting be authorized by the Holy See? Rome wisely refrained from giving instructions and let superiors judge for their subjects. Thus it was that the Jesuit General gave permission only to the Flemish Jesuits. The story is that this exception was due to the telegraph operator who left out the negative "niet" at the end of the sentence—but this is probably a legend. As for me, I was covered by my superior, Dom Capelle, who also participated in the congress. At Saint-Serge Père Kern insisted on scrupulously respecting Rome's instructions concerning interconfessional meetings. The sessions were not open to everyone, and participation was only by invitation extended to competent specialists. Nevertheless, Père Daniélou did not obtain his superior's authorization, even though he promised to give a talk. Since he had already arranged to meet Professor Jeremias, he was obliged to come to see him between the sessions. Since then he came back more than once, the last time when he was a cardinal of the Roman Church. Much has changed in twenty years.

The first Saint-Serge Study Week was a success, not only for the quality of the talks and the high standards of the sessions, but especially for the climate of fervor and evangelical simplicity that welcomed us. You weren't in the anonymous premises of an assembly: you found yourself within an authentic Christian community taking care of you. I found this climate every time I've returned to Saint-Serge with the passing years, and I'm sure to find it the next time I go back there.

I don't have the list of those invited the first time to mingle with the community of Saint-Serge. I'll give the names of those I remember: among the Protestants were Professor Jeremias and Pastor Thurian; among the Anglicans were Professors Cross and Dugmore; among the Catholics were Dom Beauduin, Dom Capelle, Dom Rousseau, Father Raes, and Msgr. Khouri-Sarkis.

The Study Weeks continued from year to year except for 1955 when, for reasons of the physical plant, the premises of Saint-Serge were not available. In the first years each person brought along the results of one's work without concern for the unity of the program. Following that, it was decided to establish a theme that would allow for deepening the comparison of different traditions. From 1961 on the *Lex orandi* series agreed to publish the sets of papers. I was asked that they be published under my name for a financially related reason. It seems that anonymous collections of articles don't sell, and an unknown name is worth more than no name at all. But it seemed impossible to me to usurp an initiative whose credit was due to Saint-Serge. I accepted on condition that the name of Bishop Cassien would also appear on the title page. Bishop Cassien, a former monk of Mount Athos, had been promoted to the episcopacy and was rector of the Institute. These printed pages, however, gave only an imperfect idea of the Weeks. The talks were just the starting place for exchanges of viewpoints and personal contacts. We are not curious people looking for entertainment but believers searching for the deepest roots of our faith in Scripture and tradition, and this common purpose creates bonds among us.

There was one year when Père Kern had a discouraging moment. Two speakers stood him up at the last minute. This wasn't catastrophic since the program was rich enough without them. But Père Kern, who was very sensitive under his austere exterior, considered this as a sign of scorn and was very much affected by it. He was mistaken. One of the two speakers was Canon Chavasse whom I knew to be incapable of making such a gesture. Besides, I learned afterwards that he had serious trouble with his health. No matter, Père Kern had an instant of bad humor, and I was its victim. He asked me to preside at the final session. I accepted quite innocently, without suspecting the trick he was going to play on me. There is a photograph of this session. You can see, to the rear on the right, the speaker's chair occupied by a rather corpulent personnage, a Swede who was speaking about the reform of the Mass in his country. On the left, at the presider's table, is seated another person whose features you cannot see. Instead of facing the audience he is turned toward the speaker with his right elbow leaning on the table and his head resting on his right hand. That person is me, but I'm not recognizable because all that you can see is my hand and my scalp. What you can't see, also, is that I am deep asleep. The applause woke me up with a start. Fortunately, I had not slept through the whole talk, and I had even taken some notes at the beginning. I was able, then, in all honesty to start a dialogue with the speaker, all the while casting nervous looks toward the back of the room. Père Kern wasn't there. I was hoping to see the outline of his tall figure in the doorway; but after a little while I realized he would not be coming back. It was useless to prolong the discussion. I thanked the speaker and tried to draw the week to a conclusion. Père Kern admitted to me afterward that he had gone to feed the ducks in the nearby park, all the while thinking with malicious joy about the look on my face when I noticed he was gone.

There was a follow-up to this episode. From then on I was asked to preside at the final session and conclude the week. At the same time we began the custom of preparing the program for the following year. This became sort of a customary law, and so much so that barely do I arrive at Saint-Serge that I'm already thinking of the next session and consulting with the representatives of the different groups to find a subject that interests everyone. At the closing session I propose the broad outline of a program to the group. From this sketch Père Kniazeff, the successor of Père Kern, puts together the definitive program during the year and invites the speakers. He does this very joyfully. These programs are rich, varied, and well-balanced.

Over the course of those twenty years we saw several workers of the first hour pass away: at Saint-Serge Père Kern, Bishop Cassien, Père Afanasieff; among the invited speakers Dom Beauduin, Dom Capelle, Professor Grondijs, and Professor Cross. We reverently keep their memory. I am the last survivor of that generation—and I've been awarded the title of patriarch!

Because of my loyalty the Theology School of Saint-Serge

granted me the great honor of conferring a doctoral degree *honoris causa* in 1968. In fact, this honor had already been proposed several years before Vatican II to me and to Père Dumont, the Dominican director of the Istina Center. We consulted each other and, after checking with our respective superiors, we had to refuse. But the situation was much different after Vatican II, and we were both very happy to accept.

I have sketched rapidly the history of the Saint-Serge Weeks. I am no prophet and cannot predict the future, but I hope the tradition continues. If old friends disappear, there are young ones who are capable of carrying on what we began. They are at Saint-Serge and among our invitees. When I became director of the Institut Supérieur de Liturgie in Paris, I led many of my students to Saint-Serge, and they gladly return there. Each year we see students from different countries arrive, eager to immerse themselves in tradition. We must live in the present and prepare for the future. The church has to be living and adapt itself to the modern world, but continuity is a condition of life. A renewed church is not a church cut off from its roots but, on the contrary, more deeply rooted in its authentic tradition. The face of the church will not be renewed by creating new divisions but by repairing those of the past. When the church is seeking its own unity, this unity will not be found in confused ideas or in facile pragmatism, but in a return to its origins. In this area Saint-Serge can and must still do good work.

13

Toward the Council

In this chapter Botte groups several topics which occurred immediately before the Second Vatican Council. He begins by describing his appointment to the Chair of Liturgy at Louvain University in 1960. Next, he describes John XXIII's convocation of the Council early in 1959 and curial reactions to it. He then turns to the organizational role of Father Annibale Bugnini in coordinating the organizational work before the Council. Finally, Botte writes about his own share in the work of three preparatory subcommittees which drafted texts on the vernacular, concelebration, and the teaching of liturgy. These drafts were debated energetically at the Council and their insights were eventually incorporated into the Constitution on the Sacred Liturgy which was issued on 4 December 1963.

Botte underscores an important conviction of his collaborators, namely, that "the role of the Council Fathers was not to approve a completely finished program ... with all the details, but to establish the general principles and orientations." This would enable us today to concur with the words written by Botte in his final chapter to the effect that "the reform is a plan for the future, and it would be a risky illusion to expect immediate, spectacular results from it." (Tr.)

T HE THREE PRECEDING CHAPTERS have sketched the history of three institutions which were born at the same time and 'with which I have had a connection: the Summer Courses organized at Louvain, the Institut Supérieur de Liturgie in Paris, and the Saint-Serge Weeks. In 1960 I accepted the Chair of Liturgy at the University of Louvain. Allow me to move back in time to explain the latter.

The School of Theology never had a liturgy course before 1911. It was certainly under the influence of the liturgical movement that Msgr. Callewaert, the liturgy professor at the Bruges major seminary, was assigned a course at the School of Theology. The university stopped functioning in 1914, and it was not till 1919 that courses began once again. Yet the mandate of Msgr. Callewaert was not renewed. I don't know the reason. Maybe Msgr. Callewaert felt that the small number of students was not worth the trip. At any rate, when the new abbot of Mont César, Dom Capelle, decided to start a public course in liturgy at the abbey, there was no liturgy course at the School of Theology. The course at the abbey was primarily aimed at our students, that is, for the Benedictines of the Belgian Congregation who took their theological studies with us, but it was open to students from the other theological schools in the city, in particular the Jesuits and the Dominicans. Dom Capelle had asked me to give some of the lectures, and this was the origin of my vocation as a liturgist. Since the courses were open to the public, students of the University attended, and yet we did no advertising there. In fact, the rare theology students who showed a desire to come to us were dissuaded by Canon Lebon, president of Holy Spirit College. This eminent patrologist never understood how the study of the prayer of the church could ever have any interest for theology. Besides, for him as well as for many of his colleagues, the liturgy was still a matter of rubrics. Still, after a few years, this disregard gave way to another principle. The University of Louvain has always been jealous of its privileges and doesn't like people to do things outside its orbit. So they created a liturgy course at the School of Theology and asked Dom Capelle to take it. Dom Capelle accepted. Nonetheless, our public courses at the abbey continued.

At first Dom Capelle's course at the University was one hour per week for one semester. It was completely optional. Furthermore, it was practically impossible to have it listed on the program of optional courses. No one was obliged to take it and, as a result, the classroom was almost deserted. Dom Capelle complained to the rector, Msgr. Ladeuze, who granted the course a second semester so that it could become an elective. Also, Msgr. Lefort, director of the Institut Orientaliste, put the course on the program for the students of the Christian Orient section. When Dom Capelle reached retirement age, he had to be replaced. It never entered Dom Capelle's mind that I should succeed him—he admitted this later on with some embarrassment. But others thought of it. In the meantime I had become director of the Institut Supérieur de Liturgie in Paris. Since this Institute was doing quite well, some professors regretted that I'd gone so far away to establish a liturgical institute. I was informed that if I were to apply for the position, I would be unanimously accepted. I answered that I wasn't interested in applying. In fact, it wasn't worth my while to accept. I was director of an international institute in Paris; I was giving my public lectures at the abbey. Why take on still another course with a registration that, after all, was rather meager? My confrere, Dom Cappuyns, who was professor of the history of medieval theology, took on the job temporarily, hoping to overcome my resistance. As a matter of fact, that was what happened. He gave classes for two years, even though he had no special competence, as he very well knew. He'd gotten himself into an unhappy situation, and in 1960 I finally accepted to get him out of it. The most students I ever had was seven, the majority coming from the Institut Orientaliste and not from the School of Theology.

In 1959 we had celebrated, as I've described, the fiftieth anniversary of the liturgical movement, and Pope John XXIII sent a message to Dom Beauduin. This took place at the beginning of July. A month or two later the pope offered a message to the world announcing that a Council would be held in the near future. I heard about this in Venice where I was giving a series of summer workshops at the Cini Foundation on San Giorgio Island.

The plans of the new pope were already known, and this caused both surprise and worry. Surprise, first of all, because John XXIII was considered a transitional pope. After a pontiff as brilliant and as criticized as Pius XII, a more low-keyed man was needed, one whose pontificate would not be too long—his age guaranteed that—and who'd give the church a few years of rest. But this "quiet father" was going to precipitate the biggest house-cleaning in the history of the church. But worry was added to the surprise. Almost everyone was hostile to the Council, for sometimes opposite reasons. The partisans of the *status quo* of the church thought there was no reason to convoke a Council since there wasn't any new heresy to condemn, as had been the case with the ancient Councils, and besides, the conciliar age was outmoded. Ease of communications made the movement of so many persons useless. Rome was perfectly informed from day to day about everything that was happening in the world and could rapidly make the necessary decisions. As for those who wished for a relaxation of discipline and some decentralization, they wondered whether the Council would be an effective remedy. Wouldn't the bishops who would be arriving from all corners of the world be invited to sign prearranged texts of the Curia which would harden some positions instead of softening them? To say the least, the idea of John XXIII did not stir up generalized enthusiasm early on.

I believe that the liturgists were the happiest over the sweet obstinancy of the pope, since the Council came at just the right time for the liturgical movement. Fifty years of study and experience had prepared for a reform. Of course it was already underway, but it was moving slowly and timidly. It still depended on the Congregation of Rites whose prefect, Cardinal Cicognani, was not a shining light. The summoning of the Council would really force Rome to adopt more effective work methods and to take more daring initiatives. The liturgists felt themselves in a position to shoulder the task. I was one of the very first to be appointed a consultor of the pre-conciliar commission. I was glad, not for my own personal reasons, but because Pères Gy and Jounel were appointed at the same time. But I noticed bemusedly that this appointment caused some disappointment to others who had not been named. One of them explained to me that this was not at all important and that these consultors would have no say. Fortunately, he was appointed a little while later, and showed praiseworthy zeal. As far as I was concerned, I wasn't worried about what I'd have to do or not have to do. I was satisfied to note that the Paris Institute was taken seriously, since its professors were among the first to be appointed.

Before discussing the projects I took part in, I want to be sure to mention my admiration for the man who organized all the work, Father Bugnini. He is one of those modest workmen who remain offstage, but without whom nothing would get done. His position as secretary was difficult and delicate. National susceptibilities had to be dealt with, while safeguarding the quality and level of the work. It was desirable, in fact, to invite liturgists of different countries to collaborate in the reform; but nationality was not a criterion of competence, and a eye had to be kept on seeing that the various problems were treated by the best qualified people. Furthermore, this would be only the first stage of the work. The role of the Council fathers was not to approve a completely finished reform that would be presented to them with all the details, but to establish the general principles and orientations for a reform. The practical application of these principles could be done only after the Council. We had to avoid getting lost in the concrete details. Rather, we had to search for the main principles for today's reform of the liturgy in the study of tradition and in pastoral experience.

I took part in three subcommittees: the vernacular, concelebration, and the teaching of liturgy.

The problem of liturgical language was arising with an ever greater sharpness and had caused some lively controversies. It is true that the discipline had eased: Rome had authorized the drafting of bilingual rituals and lectionaries in the vernacular. But this was done in the form of indults granted to local churches as departures from a general law still in force: Latin is the liturgical language of the Roman liturgy. Still, many people regarded these concessions as insufficient and, for pastoral reasons, wanted an extension of the vernacular.

Nevertheless, this viewpoint came up against an age-old tradition. The church, once it had left Palestine, adopted Greek as its mode of expression. But to the extent that the church spread, it accepted the spoken cultural languages in different areas, like Syriac and Coptic in the East. In the West the only cultural language was Latin, and it remained so during the whole of the Middle Ages. Compared to Latin, the only thing that occurred was a fragmentation among Romantic or Germanic dialects. A change in liturgical language was hardly possible before the beginning of the sixteenth century. But this coincided with the Reformation, and the Reformers took the side of the vernacular. As a result, the problem changed from one of linguistics to one of theology. The use of the vernacular allowed the Reformers to spread their ideas among the people, and maintaining Latin seemed necessary for safeguarding orthodoxy.

The intransigence of the Council of Trent is explained by circumstances, but four centuries had passed since then, and conditions had changed. Missionary expansion had to be reckoned with. The problem was no longer being raised only for the countries of old classical culture but for the young churches of Asia and Africa outside this culture. It was impossible for the Council not to examine the issue afresh.

Actually, there was a subcommittee in charge of studying the question. Its relator was Msgr. Borella of Milan and its secretary was the Dutch Franciscan, Father Brinkhof. I was one of the consultors. This subcommittee, to my knowledge, never met; but I learned from Father Brinkhof that things were at a standstill. So I took the initiative of writing a report of my own which I sent to Father Brinkhof, who mimeographed it and sent it to all the members of the subcommittee.

I first pointed out that, since the Council was ecumenical, principles valid for both East and West had to be formulated. The true tradition of the church then had to be shown by history, and the false theological arguments used previously had to be put aside, for example, the principle of the three sacred languages established by the inscription on the cross in Hebrew, Greek, and Latin. First off, Pilate had no competence to determine a sacred language. It is even a misinterpretation since the Hebrew referred to is not the language of the Old Testament but rather Aramaic, the tongue spoken at the time in Palestine. To give the passage a prophetic sense one would have to refer to living languages, not sacred ones. The inscription was supposed to be understood by all passers-by, and it was written in Aramaic, that is, the vernacular of the country; in Greek, the international tongue; and in Latin, the official language of the Empire. Latin, therefore, is no more a sacred language than is Syriac, Coptic, or Ethiopian. It is also just as incorrect to link the use of Latin to a so-called law of the arcane, as if there were a desire to hide from the people the meaning of the sacred words. Such an idea is not only foreign, but contrary to, the practice of the church in the early centuries.

The historical facts speak for themselves. As soon as the church has found in an area a cultural language possessing a written form, it has adopted that language for reading the Bible and for its liturgy. Some Eastern liturgies are celebrated today in languages as dead as Latin, but when they were adopted they were quite living. Latin is no exception. It took over throughout the West because it was the only cultural language available to the people.

Therefore there could be no objection by reason of principle to the use of the vernacular. The question before us was one of the timeliness of making a change, and only those in authority in the church could make this decision. They had to judge according to the effectiveness of the possible change, whether entirely or partially, while taking into account the missionary expansion of the church.

Msgr. Borella took the ideas from my report to draft an outline which looked very good to me. He sent this to Rome. Its arrival was acknowledged, but he was also told that his report was filed away in the archives. This meant that his text was not discussed, and the subcommittee on the vernacular had nothing left to do.

As a matter of fact, a reading of Vatican II's Constitution on the Sacred Liturgy shows that the question of liturgical language is not treated anywhere *ex professo*. It shows up only by accident, for example, in regard to the sacraments.

Who removed Msgr. Borella's report from the discussion and for what purpose? I don't know. One can only surmise. Did they want purely and simply to avoid the problem, or instead make the solution easier by avoiding a theoretical discussion which could very well have been heated and stormy? I don't see how I can answer the question for the time being.

I also belonged to the subcommission on concelebration. Dom Capelle was relator and I was secretary. The other members were the bishop of Linz, Canon Martimort, and Father Hänggi, then a professor at Freiburg in Switzerland. The only meeting was held in this city. To tell the truth, our way had been laid out for us. As I mentioned previously, the question had been treated at the international meeting held at Mont César in 1954 where no agreement was reached. The German group wanted to have silent concelebration declared valid. Since then there had been two official documents: a decree of the Holy Office, and the speech of Pius XII after the 1956 Assisi Congress requiring the recitation of the institution narrative by all the concelebrants. It was impossible for us to turn the clock back. We were the victims of the way the problem had been approached. It was raised in connection with meetings of many priests, as at a retreat. They could attend together one group Mass, but then they did not celebrate "their" Mass. So, interminable series of private Masses were organized on improvised altars. Concelebration seemed to be an easy way for all of them to say their Mass together. This is to say that it was the synchronizing of several Masses and not a collegial act of the *presbyterium.* The problem was further complicated by that of Mass stipends. Out of our discussion came a report which was more prudent than profound. It was useless to renew the experience of 1954.

The third subcommittee I belonged to was assigned to plan the teaching of liturgy. To my knowledge, it never met. But one day I received a report which offered useful recommendations: the professor was to study liturgy under all its aspects—biblical, theological, pastoral. I was completely in agreement, but it seemed to lack a bit of realism. To give courses first of all required competent professors, and nothing was envisioned for their training. I proposed an addition, namely, that future professors of liturgy be trained in specialized institutes. Perhaps this was a bit bold since there were only two institutes of this kind then in existence, the one in Paris and Saint Anselm's in Rome. Still, my request was respected and the need for special training was admitted. Beyond that, I was kept up-to-date by the papers sent to me from Rome and by what my two colleagues from the Institute in Paris, Pères Gy and Jounel, told me since they regularly attended the sessions in Rome. It seemed to me that everything was going well. Father Bugnini had adopted a good methodology. Instead of presenting the consultors with a prefabricated schema and asking them to go along with it, as was done elsewhere, he opted for making the consultors work. He realized the importance of the work accomplished by the international meetings. He had at hand teams of individuals competent in history and open to pastoral problems. Besides, these teams had been working together already for more than a decade. The Constitution on the Liturgy had to be the liturgical movement's harvest. The direction of the reform proposed to the Council Fathers was supposed to have a theological basis and rest on authentic tradition, but at the same time keep in mind pastoral needs and adapt itself to the contemporary world— in particular to watch out for the simplicity and truthfulness of the rites.

I did not attend the discussions of the Council on the schema that was presented. According to what those present told me, it was well received by the body of the Council Fathers. However, there was a surprise at the opening of the Council.

Whereas all the work was accomplished under the discreet and effective direction of Father Bugnini, the secretary, he was excluded and replaced by Father Antonelli of the Congregation of

Rites when it was time to propose the prepared schema to the Council Fathers. Strictly speaking there was nothing to find fault with here, but under the circumstances this measure must have appeared to be a falling into disfavor for Father Bugnini. Some members of the Curia were displeased with the schema, which they considered too progressive, and they directed their bad feelings against Father Bugnini. Still, this low blow did not succeed. The vote of the Council Fathers showed that the schema well responded to the wishes of the majority.

The Council Fathers were supposed to elect a floor manager from among themselves. Bishop Calewaert of Ghent was chosen. Future historians of the Council will perhaps wonder what were the reasons for this choice. I can suggest an explanation. I knew Bishop Calewaert very well, having been a classmate of his at the University of Louvain. He had no competence in matters liturgical and never took an interest in the liturgical movement. He had been present at the Congress of Lugano but, as he admitted to me, this was at the request of Cardinal Van Roey, who wanted to see the Belgian Episcopate represented there. Bishop Calewaert went as on an official assignment. But what attracted votes to his name? It was, I think, a case of mistaken identity. There had been an eminent Belgian liturgist who had almost the same name, namely, Msgr. Camille Callewaert (with two l's), the president of the Bruges seminary, about whom I spoke earlier and who died only a few years previously. The spelling difference of the names was too slight to avoid the mix-up, and I'm convinced that a good number of the Council Fathers thought they'd voted for the illustrious liturgist.

Once the Constitution on the Sacred Liturgy was approved and promulgated, the work had not ended since the Constitution contained only the principles and general directives of the reform. The principles now had to become reality, that is, we had to proceed to the reform of the different liturgical books of the Roman Rite. Normally, this task would fall under the competence of the Congregation of Rites. But the reforms called for by the Council were too extensive for the ordinary personnel of the congregation to meet the task. Consequently, a new structure was created whose function was to carry out the Council's decisions.

14

The Consilium

Here Botte outlines the structure, makeup, and work methods of this important commission chartered by Paul VI on 29 February 1964 to put the liturgical reform ordered by Vatican II on the map. He introduces the reader to the group he led as a relator or floor manager for the revision of the first part of the Pontifical, namely, the book containing those liturgies presided over by a bishop. We are treated to a look at one unfortunate case of "systematic obstructionism" and occasional instances of "external (read 'papal') intervention."

After five years' work this commission with its remaining projects was subsumed by Paul VI into a new Congregation for Divine Worship by a decree dated 8 May 1969. (Tr.)

T HE IMPLEMENTATION OF THE REFORM prescribed by Vatican II was entrusted to a new organism, parallel to the Congregation of Rites and called the *Consilium ad exsequendam Constitutionem de Sacra Liturgia* (Commission for the Implementation of the Constitution on the Sacred Liturgy). I will call it simply the Commission. Its president was then the Cardinal Archbishop of Bologna, Cardinal Lercaro; its secretary was Father Annibale Bugnini. This was only fitting reparation for the falling from favor he had sustained at the beginning of the Council. Father Bugnini demonstrated the same organizational qualities he had shown during the preparation of the Constitution on the Liturgy.

The Commission was made up of two different groups. First, there were forty members as such—mostly cardinals and bishops—who had a deliberative vote. Then there was the group of consultors, more numerous and given the task of preparing the work. This group naturally included most of those who belonged to the pre-conciliar Commission, but there were a lot of new faces. The ostensible aim was to see that all viewpoints and countries be represented. From Mont César there were four of us: Abbot Rombaut Van Doren, Dom Placide Bruylants, Dom François Vandenbroecke, and myself. The consultors were divided into several groups with a well-defined area for each. Presiding over each group was a relator who was to organize its work as best he could. This wasn't always easy because the consultors were scattered all over the place. I was relator for the first part of the Pontifical, and my collaborators lived in Aachen, Münster in Westphalia, Strasbourg, Paris, and Rio de Janeiro.

Periodically full meetings were held in Rome. These included two sessions: one for the consultors, another for the members as such. In the former each relator was invited in turn to submit the results of his group's work to the full body of consultors present. Since this critique was to be based on a written text, the relator was supposed to send to the secretariat beforehand a report which was copied and supplied to all the consultors. Most often the meetings were held in the Palazzo Santa Marta, behind Saint Peter's Basilica, in the main room on the ground floor. We sat at a series of large tables. Cardinal Lercaro took his place on the end at a small table, with Father Bugnini at his right and the relator at his left. The latter read his report line by line and responded to the questions and objections raised. All could speak and propose corrections. A discussion ensued, and attempts were made to find a solution which satisfied the majority. And yet the only function of these consultors' meetings, which lasted a week, was that of preparing for the meetings of the cardinal and bishop members of the Commission, who alone had a deliberative vote. After a few days' rest, the bishops' session then opened. This time it was the bishops who sat at the tables. The consultors could attend these sessions. They sat where they could on chairs along the walls. They had the right to speak, but they did not vote. Seated on Cardinal Lercaro's left, the relator again read his report as it was revised by the observations and corrections proposed by the consultors. When the discussion could not reach an agreement, recourse was had to a vote. Most of the time this was by a show of hands. In more serious cases the voting was in secret. It was the relator who was to move the question. At least this was customary when Cardinal Lercaro was president of the Commission. But when he had been replaced by Cardinal Gut, the latter once wanted to propose a vote instead of me. I firmly opposed it, and he had to withdraw his motion. After a draft had been examined part-by-part in this way, the full text was considered as a whole, and the final vote of the Commission was considered definitive. The draft could then be submitted for the pope's approval.

I feel it necessary to cover all these details because it is important to know how the liturgical reform was done. It caused much public discussion which sometimes degenerated into partisan quarrels. Recently I came across the opinion of a well-known Dominican in a Paris newspaper. For him the new liturgy is the work of a few uncultured leftists who are ignorant of tradition. I am sorry that I have to contradict the good father, but the majority of the consultors I met seemed rather cultured and, in all events, they knew liturgical tradition very well. As for their political opinions, I can't say anything because we never discussed politics. Various viewpoints were found among the consultors, but it would be wrong to believe that the group was divided into a right wing hostile to all change and a left wing ready to turn everything upside down. Almost all of them were convinced there was a need for a reform, but didn't always agree about the means. They discussed seriously in order to find a solution, and it often happened that close to unanimous agreement was reached after the discussion.

If the liturgical reform is not a masterpiece, we must at least recognize that it is the result of an honest and conscientious effort. I encountered only one case of systematic obstructionism. There was this important personage, a type of windbag who was also supercilious. When he was on hand he saw himself as the only center of attention. He grabbed the microphone, took upon himself a review of all the objections that could have been made, added some of his own, and said anything that came to mind. His tactics were clear: he tried to have the work drag on as long as possible. Unfortunately for him, he didn't know how to judge how far was too far, and one fine day he cooked his own goose. I proposed to the Commission the text of an address which we had composed for the ordination of a bishop. Hardly had I finished my explanation than I heard the peremptory remark: "The old address was better." The speaker wanted to develop his idea, but I grabbed the mike in front of me and cut him off by asking where this address was found in the Pontifical. He wanted to go off on a tangent, but I brought him back to the question. He gazed at me with a stunned look. I added: "Don't look, it's not worth your time—there never was an address for the ordination of a bishop in the Pontifical." A little discreet laughter was heard, followed by silence. Our address was approved without any difficulty.

As I mentioned, the work of the Commission was based on the written reports of different groups of consultors. How were these reports drawn up? The relator had the task of organizing the work, and not all the relators proceeded in the same way. All I can do is indicate what I did as relator of my group.

We were in charge of the reform of the first book of the Pontifical, that is, mainly the ordinations. At the outset I had five consultors. First, the secretary, Father Kleinheyer (then professor at the Aachen seminary), was the youngest, but he had just gained attention by an outstanding thesis on priestly ordination in the Roman Rite. Then there was Père Vogel, professor at Strasbourg, who had taken over from Msgr. Andrieu the publication of the *Ordines Romani* and the *Romano-Germanic Pontifical.* Also Father Lengeling, who at that time was professor of liturgy at Münster in Westphalia. He is now dean of the School of Theology. Also Père Jounel who was and still is professor at the Institut Supérieur de Liturgie in Paris. Finally there was a Brazilian prelate, Msgr. Nabuco, the author of a *Commentary on the Roman Pontifical,* who died a few years ago. He was not a great help to us since he did not adapt himself to our method of working, namely, by correspondence. He did not respond to the questions asked of him, but when he was in Europe he pestered me to call a meeting of the group. Unfortunately, the others weren't available at those times, and I was not able to comply with his requests. Later on we co-opted Père Lécuyer, a professor at the French seminary in Rome and now Superior General of the Holy Spirit Fathers.

The greatest part of the work, then, was done by correspondence. I wrote the first draft with Father Kleinheyer, the secretary. Geographically we were close enough to each other: from Louvain to Aachen it is only a two hour trip by car or train, so we were able to meet easily. This draft was then sent to the other consultors who communicated to us their critiques and remarks. Then we tried to modify the draft in light of these remarks and resubmitted it for their criticisms. At one point we began a revision by three of us: the secretary, Professor Lengeling, and myself. After we sent out our results to the others, we had some general meetings. These were not many and were always brief. I remember that for the last one we had planned on two days in Paris, but we already finished up on the first day.

The other group leaders proceeded differently and held many meetings which were often very lengthy. It's not my place to criticize them, but I can state that we were the first to present a definitive schema to be approved by the Commission and by the pope. The reason for this, I believe, is due to the particular competence of the consultors given me, and most especially that of the secretary. The reports we submitted to the Commission included not only the text of the new ritual but sets of explanatory notes. These notes were written up by the secretary with remarkable care. All the changes that we envisioned were justified ahead of time—something that made the discussion easier. I have fond memories of this work we did together. There was neither right nor left among us, only the same desire to respond to the directives given by Vatican II.

I have described the normal functioning of the Commission. I must add that on occasion it was disturbed by external intervention. This wasn't the fault of Cardinal Lercaro or of Father Bugnini—both of whom were always fair. Thus in the first report I submitted on ordinations, I proposed the suppression of the minor orders with the exception of lector. I was told that my report would go nowhere if I maintained this position. I wasn't informed as to the source of the opposition, but there is good reason to believe it was Paul VI. There were other cases where people unhappy with a decision of the Commission tried to have it undone by recourse to the pope.

One day we were surprised to learn that Cardinal Lercaro was relieved of the Commission's directorship and replaced by Cardinal Gut. This was doubly scandalous. The first reason was the way in which Cardinal Lercaro was removed. He had offered his resignation on account of age, but it was refused. He filled his functions to the general satisfaction of all. Then, one fine day a messenger came to notify him that his resignation was accepted.

This had nothing to do with liturgy but with politics. No less scandalous was the appointment of Cardinal Gut. He was a man who was worn-out and perfectly incompetent in matters liturgical. He recognized this, and yet it did not keep him from making untimely interventions about questions he didn't understand at all. Fortunately, Father Bugnini remained as secretary and sought to limit the damage.

The Commission was disbanded before finishing its work. A while ago I received a letter from Rome thanking me for my good and faithful service and telling me the Commission no longer existed. Henceforth the Congregation for Divine Worship, successor of the Congregation of Rites, was given the job of completing the work. However, a few consultors of the Commission were retained as consultors of the Congregation for Divine Worship and Father Bugnini, made a titular archbishop, is secretary of this congregation.

How does one explain that the reform remains unfinished and that its follow-up evidently moves on so slowly? The extent of the undertaking and its difficulty could be pointed to. Maybe all the work groups did not have the same pace, but that's not enough. Why, for example, did the ritual of confirmation have to wait three years before its publication? This wasn't the Commission's fault. On the contrary, the reason is to be found in the fact that not enough confidence was placed in the Commission. Before a schema receives definitive approval from the pope, it must be submitted to the censorship of several Roman congregations, in particular those for the Faith, for the Sacraments, and for Rites. Everything could be called into question, as I saw with the ordination rites. I will return to this episode further on. You can understand how this method puts a brake on things, not allowing the work to proceed at a normal pace. This must also be kept in mind when judging the Commission's work. The texts that were promulgated were not always exactly the same as those voted on by the Commission. People, sometimes of debatable competence and out of touch with these texts, manipulated them.

I needn't apologize here for the liturgical reform. Like every human endeavor it is imperfect, and certain points can be criticized. But I must pay tribute to those who organized the work of the Commission, Cardinal Lercaro and Father Bugnini. Cardinal Lercaro was always a model president, warm to all, impartial, and respectful of all opinions. He might be reproached a bit for being too low-keyed and too careful not to influence the vote of the group. As for Archbishop Bugnini, he was the equal of what he'd been during the preparations for Vatican II, organizing the work while himself staying in the background.

While preparations were underway for Vatican II, I avoided moving around. But when the Commission was established, I was often obliged to stay in Rome in order to speak before the group. These visits were as short as possible. As there were two sessions back-to-back, I received permission to speak on the last day of the former and on the first day of the latter. My excuse was that after three days I turned anti-clerical, and after a week I risked losing my faith. It was only a joke, but I must say that I did not bear up well under the Roman atmosphere. I like Italy a lot though, and have fine memories of time spent in Verona, Florence, and Venice. But Rome was something else. There was too much red, purple, and cassocks. I stayed at the Pensionato Romano, a large building six stories high, located on the via Transpontina, not far from the Vatican. It was comfortable and meticulously clean; but the cooking was insipid, and the atmosphere purely clerical. My only break was to eat my meals in the little public restaurants on the nearby streets where I felt more at ease.

All the same, I don't want to leave the impression that I have only bad memories of these visits. I met old friends there and came to know new ones, with whom I have had the joy of working for the service of the church. We did so conscientiously, without any partisan spirit. We will have to wait for hindsight to judge properly the value of the reform. I am convinced that the judgment of history will be favorable.

I must still speak more in detail concerning some of the reforms in which I was personally involved: the ordination rites, the Mass, and confirmation.

15

Ordination Rites

Given the brevity of the remarks in the conciliar document on the liturgy about revising "both the ceremonies and texts of the ordination rites" (par. 76), it was only natural that the starting point of Botte's work group was a careful examination of the Roman tradition. A whole series of choices made in "comparative liturgy" fashion, and based on extensive knowledge of ancient and medieval texts, awaited Botte and the other experts. He sets out his position on what were called "minor orders" in energetic terms, leaving no room for doubt about his thought on the matter. (Tr.)

T HE FIRST BOOK OF THE ROMAN PONTIFICAL contains the consecrations of persons reserved to the bishop. This is the area where the group for which I was the relator began its work. Earlier I described my work with a team of particularly competent consultors. The first report I sent to the Commission included a general outline embracing all the orders, major and minor. I foresaw the suppression of several of the latter since they no longer responded to real usage. In his reply Father Bugnini let me know that, if I maintained this position, my report would go nowhere. Only one thing could be done: leave aside for a while the minor orders and begin with the major orders.

The reform of these rites posed some ticklish problems. The Pontifical took shape progressively, from the fifth to the end of the thirteenth centuries, to a great extent outside Rome. It contained elements of very different origin and value. The essential element, that is, the laying on of hands, was somewhat buried under a pile of secondary rites. Furthermore, certain formulas were inspired by medieval theology and needed correction. For example, the theologians of the Middle Ages considered the handing over of the paten and chalice to be the essential rite of ordination to the priesthood. Now, this was not compatible with the Apostolic Constitution *Sacramentum Ordinis* of Pius XII which had reestablished the primacy of the laying on of hands. The rite of handing over the paten and chalice could be retained, but not the accompanying formula: "Receive the power to celebrate Mass for the living and the dead." The power to celebrate Mass is given to the priest by the imposition of hands alone. Besides, the text was loaded with questionable symbolism: for example, the mitre as symbolizing the two horns of Moses as he came down from the mountain. The investiture ceremonies were interminable. The instructions given by the Council prescribed restoring simplicity and genuineness to the rites, so that the rites and prayers might catechize the people on holy orders. For this reason we had set aside the radical solution of restoring the ordinations to the fifth century state by suppressing the secondary rites added on through the ages. When judiciously chosen, these rites could be an element of catechesis. So we took the Roman Pontifical as it stood for our point of departure, and critiqued it to determine what could be retained of the Roman tradition. I cannot give all the details of the work here, but I would simply like to dwell on some of the more important problems.

The main one was the formula for the ordination of a bishop. The text in the Pontifical was comprised of two parts. The first was derived from some old strictly Roman sacramentaries, the Leonine and the Gregorian. They articulated only one idea: the bishop was the high priest of the New Testament. In the Old Testament the high priest was consecrated by anointing with oil and clothing with precious vestments. In the New it was the anointing of the Holy Spirit and the ornament of virtues. The literary form of this section did not make up for its poor content. The typology insisted exclusively on the cultic role of the bishop and left aside his apostolic ministry. The second part was a long interpolation found for the first time in the Gelasian Sacramentary. It consists of a jumbled series of scriptural quotations, most of which—but not all—are linked to the apostolic ministry. This interpolation of the Gelasian did not suffice to reestablish the balance. Could we, after Vatican II, retain such a poor formula? Was it possible to correct and improve the text?

I didn't see how we could make a coherent whole out of the two badly matched parts of the formula. Should we create a new prayer from start to finish? I felt myself incapable of this. It's true that some amateurs could be found who would be willing to attempt it—some people feel they have a special charism for composing liturgical formulas—but I don't trust these amateurs. Wouldn't it be more reasonable to seek a formula in the oriental rites that could be adapted? An examination of the oriental rites led my attention to a text I knew well, the prayer in the Apostolic Tradition of Saint Hippolytus.

The first time I proposed this to my colleagues they looked at me in disbelief. They found Hippolytus' formula to be excellent, but they didn't believe it had the slightest chance of being accepted. I told them that I perhaps had a way of getting it accepted. If I was paying attention to this text it wasn't because I had just finished a critical edition of it, but because my study of the oriental rites made me notice that the formula always survived under more evolved forms. Thus, in the Syrian Rite the prayer for the patriarch's ordination was none other than the one in the *Testamentum Domini*, a reworking of the Apostolic Tradition. The same is true for the Coptic Rite where the prayer for the bishop's ordination is close to that of the Apostolic Constitutions, another reworking of Hippolytus' text. The esssential ideas of the Apostolic Tradition can be found everywhere. Reusing the old text in the Roman Rite would affirm a unity of outlook between East and West on the episcopacy. This was an ecumenical argument. It was decisive.

I had provided the fathers with a synoptic table of the different texts with a brief commentary. The discussion was lively, and I understand why. What finally obtained a favorable vote was, I think, Père Lécuyer's intervention. He had published in the *Nouvelle revue théologique* a short article showing how the text of the Apostolic Tradition agreed with the teaching of the ancient Fathers. During the session, when it was time to vote on this issue, he made a plea which convinced those who were wavering. Afterward we invited him to join our work group, and he was a great help to us by his theological competence and knowledge of the Fathers.

Another problem was that of the addresses to the candidates. These were found in the Pontifical for all the orders except the episcopacy. They were drafted at the end of the thirteenth century by Durandus of Mende. Why did he not compose one for the ordination of a bishop? We don't know, but the question came up: wouldn't it be desirable to have an address at the beginning of this ordination? It was the hope of the Council that the ordination rite be a catechesis for the people. We believed we were responding to the Council's directives by providing an address given by the first consecrator. In our first draft there was only a simple rubric indicating the moment when it was to be made, for our understanding was that the person speaking would improvise it. Therefore, we had not drafted any text. The bishops of the Commission asked us—with an insistence that surprised us—to draft a formula which could at least serve as a model. So I asked Professor Lengeling to compose an address inspired by the teachings of Vatican II. He did this very carefully. It was an excellent synthesis of the Council's teaching: each sentence was backed up by precise references. However, since the conciliar style is not particularly elegant, I tried to give a more harmonious literary shape to the text. I don't know if I succeeded, but at least I am sure that I did not misrepresent the drafter's thought since he agreed with me.

For the presbyterate and the diaconate we had the addresses written by Durandus of Mende. Although we retained some particularly happy formulas from them, it first of all seemed necessary to rely also on the teaching of Vatican II.

The addresses are only models from which the bishop can draw inspiration. Experience has shown that the bishops' insistence on requiring these models was a sign of wisdom. After the promulgation of the ritual I received reports about first experiences with it. The very first came from a Benedictine concerning a bishop's ordination in Africa. My confrere collected the criticisms he had heard. The most serious was the reflection of two archbishops who had found a pathetic doctrinal weakness in the address. I thanked my confrere and requested some further information. After more inquiry he replied that the address concerned was a composition of the consecrating bishop and had nothing to do with the one in the new Pontifical. Some time later I heard on the radio an address given at an ordination in Belgium. It was trite and superficial, a ceremonial discourse and not an instruction for the people who didn't known anything more after than before about the role of the episcopacy. This is a shame because there is some strange confusion in this area, not only among the laity but also among many priests. Still, Vatican II must be credited with reevaluating the role of the episcopacy, and it gives clear and firm teaching about this role.

The final point that presented us with a problem was the examination which precedes the ordination of the bishop. This is an old tradition which was kept by the Pontifical. The one consecrating asked a series of questions of the candidate before the people. Undoubtedly this venerable custom should be kept, but the examination aimed at the orthodoxy of the candidate in light of heresies today having only historical interest. We thought it preferable to have the examination cover the commitment of the bishop to the church and his people. I drafted a questionnaire which I submitted for review to my consultors. We proposed it to the Commission which received it well and helped us finalize it. It serves as a useful complement to the address of the consecrator.

It seemed to us that such an examination would also be useful for the ordination of a priest and of a deacon. This is an innovation which seems to answer the Council's wish that the rites be meaningful and serve as a catechesis for the people.

I can't give the details of the changes we made so that the true nature and simplicity of the rites would be apparent. I would only point out the suppression, in the ordination of a priest, of the second imposition of hands which occurred near the end of the ceremony. This was a very late custom, unknown to the ancient Roman tradition. Its necessity for the validity of the ordination was doubted as well, but jurisprudence required that it be made up if omitted. I witnessed a very strange case. The first ordination Bishop Van Roey (the archbishop of Malines) did took place at the Abbey of Saint-André. Well, when he came to the final imposition of hands he very distinctly said "Accipe spiritum meum" rather than the traditional formula "Accipe Spiritum Sanctum." Nothing was said to Bishop Van Roey, but after his departure people asked what they ought to do. The authorities consulted declared that this laying on of hands had to be supplied. So they took the newly ordained priests to the bishop's palace in Bruges where the bishop began again the laying on of hands with the correct formula. Such cases will no longer occur since this second imposition has been suppressed.

The outline for the ordination of the bishop, priest, and deacon was the first to be definitively approved by the Commission, and it was passed on to the pope. First of all, it was delayed for months because of details. We had suppressed the singing of the *Veni creator* at the ordination of a bishop because we couldn't keep it in its original place. It was sung immediately after the laying on of the hands, when it was time for the anointing of the candidate. This was a misrepresentation since it led to the belief that the Spirit had not yet come and that the essential rite was beginning. But the only essential rite, the imposition of hands, had already been completed. The Commission by a large majority approved our suggestion, but a consultor dissatisfied with this decision directly contacted the pope who took the matter to heart. We had to find another place for the *Veni creator*.

Thereafter we decided to use the new rite on the occasion of the ordination of Bishop Hänggi, bishop-elect of Basel. But before obtaining the pope's definitive approval, the text still had to be submitted for review to the appropriate Roman congregations. This is why I was called to Rome to appear before a commission composed of representatives of the Congregation for the Faith, the Congregation of the Sacraments, and the Congregation of Rites.

The latter congregation proceeded in an entirely correct fashion: it sent me a series of written remarks which I had time to examine. Some looked well-advised to me, and I immediately agreed to them. Others were less so, but I was able to prepare a reply. Unfortunately, the other two congregations did not have the same attitude, and their representatives waited to get into the meeting to raise loads of unforseen objections. The representative from the Congregation of the Faith proved particularly zealous in dissecting the text and asking for corrrections. As banal an expression as "celebratio mysteriorum" was suspect because it could be regarded as approving the theories of Dom Casel. As a result we were not moving ahead. Perhaps this was fortunate, in a certain way, since for the time being it limited the damage to a small part of the text. But on the other hand if we continued at this pace and with the same method, I didn't see where it would all end, or, especially what would be left of our draft since everything was being challenged. This never would have happened with Cardinal Lercaro, but Cardinal Gut was incapable of leading the discussion and, when he did intervene, it was generally misinterpreted. Father Bugnini was visibly ill-at-ease, but he was intimidated by the cardinal's attitude. We couldn't continue on in this way.

I managed to keep my cool during the first meeting, but afterwards I had one of the most beautiful fits of anger in my life. I quite frankly told Cardinal Gut and Father Bugnini that if this should go on in the same way and in the same spirit, I'd pack my bags and return home. The commission had before it a draft which had required several years' work by specialists. It had been revised and corrected several times by about forty consultors of the Commission. It had been examined and approved by about forty cardinals and bishops. And, at the last minute everything had to be changed and new solutions improvised at a moment's notice on the advice of half-a-dozen incompetent bureaucrats. No lay institution could survive with such work methods.

I don't know how things were worked out, but I'm fairly certain that Father Bugnini found a diplomatic solution. He knew I'd given no empty threat, and he himself was exasperated by the procedure. As a matter of fact the person from the Congregation of the Faith who really got on our nerves had disappeared by the next session, and I've never seen him since. At the beginning of the second meeting I ventured to tell the representatives of the congregations, except for the Congregation of Rites which had sent its remarks beforehand, what I thought of their method. The review then moved ahead by leaps and bounds, and it was over by the end of the meeting. The text was ready for the ordination of Bishop Hänggi.

Once the problem of major orders was taken care of, we then had to tackle that of minor orders. I was kept from speaking about this in my first report, but nothing kept me from stating the problem, as a private individual, in a magazine article. I laid out my position in *Questions liturgiques et paroissiales*. I honestly warned my superior, Dom Baudouin de Bie, that this article would probably be poorly welcomed in Rome and that he might have some difficulties over it. Nonetheless, he gave his full approval.

My opinion was—and still is—that the minor orders no longer correspond to reality today, and they are nothing more than a juridical fiction. The office of porter is no longer exercised by clerics, and the exorcists can't exorcise anything or anyone. The office of lector, still corresponding to actual usage, can be retained, but this order should be confered on those who really exercise it in most churches and not on clerics who remain in their seminaries. Finally, the order of acolyte has been exercised for centuries by young men or young children. It is ridiculous to confer it on seminarians at the time they are going to cease exercising it (on the eve of the subdiaconate), while they have served Mass for many years. The functions are divorced from the orders. As for the reasons adduced in favor of retaining the minor orders, they do not stand up to serious scrutiny. People speak of a venerable tradition dating back to the first centuries of the church. This is false. All this legislation rests on an apocryphal document, a false decretal of the eighth century, attributed to Pope Caius in the third century. The fathers of the Council of Trent believed in its authenticity, but this is no longer possible in the days of Vatican II. The documents present another picture. The minor orders corresponded to real functions, useful to the community, without those who performed them aspiring to the presbyterate. It is true that before reaching the presbyterate one had to pass through one or another lower stage. However, these were effective probation periods in real functions, and not a fictitious passage through all the orders. It's probable, by the way, that the orders of porter and exorcist had fallen into disuse in Rome after the fifth century. Another argument in favor of the minor orders was that they served as a good preparation for the presbyterate. Perhaps this was true fifty years ago, but is no longer so today. Young people are more demanding than we were at their age, and they're right. They do not gladly accept customs that seem inauthentic to them and that smack of fiction. And they stand in the spirit of Vatican II which has asked us to depict the true nature of the rites.

By publishing my article I hoped to stir up a discussion which would move the question forward. This didn't happen at all. Those partisan to minor orders didn't respond, doubtlessly because they didn't have much to reply. Those who shared my opinion maintained a prudent silence. When the problem was presented before the Commission, there was a touchy situation. Normally the question fell under the competence of the group for which I was the relator, but I had taken a public stand and couldn't be expected to change my mind. On the other hand, if I presented a report along the same lines as my article, I would run up against the same veto which had stopped my first report. To escape this awkward position, a new commission, presided over by the bishop of Leghorn, was created. I was invited to join, but I declined. I knew in advance they were looking for one of those diplomatic solutions which are supposed to satisfy everyone and which satisfy no one. There are four minor orders. Some want to keep them, others want to abolish them. They meet halfway: two will be abolished, two will be retained. And this is exactly what happened. They proposed keeping two orders, the one of porter which would be conferred on sacristans, and that of acolyte for seminarians. When this draft was presented to the Commission, I ventured to ask the bishops present if they were prepared to confer the order of porter on the sacristans in their diocese. My question was met with laughter, which was enough to show the lack of realism in this draft. That is as far as things went.

A few years ago I received a letter from Cardinal Samoré, prefect of the Congregation of Sacraments. He was asking my opinion on a problem presented to him by a letter from the pope's secretariat, a copy of which he sent me. The bishop of Rottenburg was supposed to ordain eleven married deacons, and he requested the pope to dispense with tonsure, minor orders, and the subdiaconate. Given the urgency, the pope granted the dispensation by telegram, but he was asking the cardinal to provide him with a report about what should be done in similar cases. In his letter Cardinal Samoré informed me that the Congregation of the Sacraments saw no problem with the abrogation of minor orders which no longer meant anything of interest for the life of the church. So I sent the cardinal a report in which I proposed that the subdiaconate be retained as the only minor order. It had been removed from the list of major orders by the Apostolic Constitution *Pontificalis Romani,* and, by that fact, no longer bound one to celibacy. On the other hand, this order is universal and has proper liturgical functions. I received Cardinal Samoré's gratitude with a check of ten thousand lire [approximately sixteen dollars in 1964]. Then silence ensued for a while.

One fine day I received the draft of a decree whose essentials can be summed up in a few words. The orders of porter and of exorcist would be abolished. The orders of lector and acolyte would be retained, but they could be conferred only on those preparing for the presbyterate. The subdiaconate would be abolished, but the functions of the subdeacon would be performed by the acolyte "as occurs in the East from long ago."

This was evidently a diplomatic solution similar to the one

which had been proposed to the Commission. The abolition of porter and exorcist was imperative, and it was astonishing how long we had to wait till this was noticed. Retaining lectors was justified if this order could be conferred on those who habitually carry out its functions; but if ordination as lector is reserved to clerics confined to their seminary, we fall back into a pure fiction. It's the same for the acolyte. It is evident that functions proper to the acolyte will continue to be exercised by children or youngsters. But what really goes beyond my understanding is what was said about the subdiaconate. This is an ancient and universal order. The subdeacon has his own vestment, the tunic, and some well-defined functions: he reads the epistle at the Solemn Mass, he assists the priest at the altar, he carries the cross in processions. These functions still exist, but the order is abolished and the functions transferred to the acolyte who thus becomes something like a one-man orchestra, entrusted with missions that are mutually incompatible. And the appeal made to the custom of the Eastern Rite tops it all off. It's impossible to entrust the subdeacon's functions to the acolyte in the East for the simple reason that there is no order of acolyte. The truth is that the subdiaconate has remained a minor order in the East. Only a misunderstanding can account for this strange arrangement. In the usage of the Latin Rite the subdiaconate is linked to the commitment to celibacy. The author of the text undoubtedly wanted to avoid committing young men prematurely to this obligation, but he did not realize that this obligation no longer existed. Perhaps this was somewhat my fault. In the draft of the Constitution *Pontificalis Romani,* which I prepared with Père Lécuyer, we softened the reduction of the subdiaconate to the rank of a minor order and its canonical consequences. We didn't speak explicitly of the subdiaconate, but simply declared that from now on only the episcopacy, the presbyterate, and the diaconate would be considered major orders. Canonically this is perfectly clear: it is evident that the subdiaconate is no longer a major order; and by this very fact the obligation of celibacy lapses since it was imposed—in terms of canon law—only because the subdiaconate was included in major orders. But a superficial reader could have overlooked this.

This draft decree was sent to the episcopal conferences for their information. I don't think it stirred up much enthusiasm.

The preceding lines were written on 9 September 1972. On the eleventh of the same month I received a letter from Cardinal

Samoré accompanying a pontifical document which was due to be promulgated on the fourteenth. This was a motu proprio of Paul VI settling the problem of minor orders. It was not without some apprehension that I perused the document, but I was quickly reassured. The perspective changed completely. They abandoned juridical fiction so as to return to the life and pastoral activity of the church. In the strict sense, there are no more minor orders. Those of porter, exorcist, and subdeacon have been abolished. As for lector and acolyte, these have been kept but are no longer counted among the clerical orders. They are simply ministries, that is, services which can normally be entrusted to lay people who do not aspire to the presbyterate. Certainly it's fitting that seminarians fill these ministries, but this is accidental. These ministries have a value in themselves for the life of each church, and their functions have been broadened: the lector becomes the animator of the asembly; the acolyte fills the function of the subdeacon and becomes an extraordinary minister of communion. You can see how pastors in parishes can take advantage of these new arrangements. My only regret is that the title of acolyte was preferred to that of subdeacon since, unlike the acolyte, the subdiaconate is found all over, in the East as well as in the West. But, when all is said and done, this is just a question of semantics.

16

Reform of the Mass

Botte continues, informing his readers of the travails of the *Consilium's* work group on the reform of the Mass mandated by the Constitution on the Sacred Liturgy (pars. 50-58). He links his narrative to the previous international meetings described in Chapter 9: years after their debates were over, we see that a realistic flow of give-and-take still had to guide both the discussions and the decision-making of the Commission. Botte points out the active role played by Pope Paul VI in following some developments of this group. He leaves us a firsthand version of how that enormous shift in Roman Rite usage occurred whereby the Roman Church received three other eucharistic prayers as companions to the Roman Canon. (Tr.)

T HE PROBLEM OF THE REFORM of the Roman Mass was treated at the first international meeting in 1951 at the Abbey of Maria Laach. This was a private meeting organized by the Trier Institute with the collaboration of the Paris Pastoral Liturgy Center. No representatives of the hierarchy or of the Roman authorities were present. Among those invited were the two best historians of the Mass: Father Jungmann and Dom Capelle. There was no doubt that the Roman Mass was in need of reform. The missal of Pius V represented a form of the liturgy established at the end of the thirteenth century, but it contained elements of differing ages and origins—like the old cathedrals which bore traces of different styles added on through the ages. If there was agreement in principle, the same was not true as to the details. Two points in particular were stumbling blocks, and I mention them here because they were discussed again after the Council.

The first and most important was that of the canon of the Mass. Father Jungmann gave a critique of it and proposed some structural reforms. Thus, the prayer for the church and the pope of the *Te igitur* would be suppressed since it would repeat the use of the prayer of intercession which would be restored before the offertory. I defended the Roman Canon. Perhaps it is not a masterpiece. It has its defects. And yet it is a venerable text, one which can't be treated nonchalantly. Aside from some slight corrections of the ninth century, it had remained just as Saint Gregory left it at the end of the sixth century. For more than thirteen centuries it has been at the heart of the eucharistic piety of Western Christianity. The theologians of the Middle Ages respected it almost like a sacred text, and they refrained from placing their own ideas in it. They accepted it like a given element of tradition. To correct it would require great discretion and some serious reasons. The proposed rearrangements, then, were arbitrary and disfigured the text without improving it. Everything stopped at this point for the time being.

Another area we were not agreed upon was the problem of the penitential act. In the ordinary of the Mass the celebrant and his servers began with a confession of sins. Originally this was a private preparation that did not include the people since it took place during the singing of the *Introit* and the *Kyrie*. But the liturgical movement had introduced the use of the dialogue Mass in which the people took part in the confession of sins. Now, some pastors attested to the faithful's attachment to this practice, and they desired that it be included in the Solemn Mass. There was no reason for rejecting this suggestion a priori. The difficulty was to find the place and form for this penitential act. Several solutions were proposed, but none received general approval.

These problems would resurface after the Council, but it is good to notice that they had been raised for a long time and that they had been carefully studied by liturgists.

The distribution of work in the Commission was based on the division of the liturgical books. But the missal was too large a book for only one working group to study in its entirety. So, there were several commissions according to the different parts of the missal: the calendar, lectionary, prayers and prefaces, Holy Week. The group assigned to the ordinary of the Mass was the most important of these.

The relator of this commission was Msgr. Wagner, the director of the Trier Liturgical Institute who organized and presided at the Maria Laach meeting in 1951. I wasn't a member of this group at the beginning, and I don't know how he organized its work—the information I have is second-hand. It wasn't very much, anyway. His group of consultors was more numerous than mine and less homogeneous. In spite of some rather long and frequent meetings, the work didn't seem to progress rapidly. The first time I took part personally was by chance. One day when I was visiting Rome Msgr. Wagner was supposed to give his report to the Commission. I was invited and joined in the discussion. It so happened that the topic was the canon. Msgr. Wagner presented a draft that took its inspiration from the ideas of Father Jungmann which I spoke about earlier in connection with the 1951 meeting. It contained some arbitrary modifications, and you wondered whether this was change just for the sake of change. The draft met with strong opposition, even from people very open to reform. An impasse had been reached.

Some time afterward, while I was in Trier with my working group, Msgr. Wagner invited me one evening to a symposium with Professor Vogel. As we were drinking an excellent Moselle wine, he shared a secret with us: he had been summoned to see Paul VI who had entrusted to him the drafting of three new eucharistic prayers to be used concurrently with the Roman Canon. To prepare these he undertook the project of gathering together all the ancient eucharistic prayers. This was the origin of the collection *Prex eucharistica*, since edited by Bishop Hänggi and Miss Pahl. The pope's initiative was unexpected, and you might wonder who inspired it. Msgr. Wagner thought that perhaps it was Père Bouyer who had been granted a private audience a few days earlier. This didn't seem plausible to me since the two audiences were too close together, and it's improbable that the pope would have made such a decision without long reflection. There is, perhaps, another explanation, but it is to be sought elsewhere.

The Dutch, who were impatiently waiting for a reform which

wasn't coming, made the first move and mass-produced a number of eucharistic prayers. Faced with this anarchy, Cardinal Alfrink took the initiative by having a collection made which contained a Dutch translation of the Roman Canon and six new eucharistic prayers. He submitted this collection to be judged by the Holy See and made a commitment to end the anarchy if three of the new texts would be approved. A special commission of cardinals and two consultors (Father Bugnini and myself) was appointed. The first of the new texts was the canon of Father Oosterhuis which was very successful in Holland and Flanders. Its indisputable literary qualities did not make up for its theological ambiguities. Jesus was an "unforgettable man." The text didn't say Jesus was only this, and there was no denial of his divinity. No dogma was denied, but dogmas ended up being shelved. It was difficult to see this prayer as an expression of authentic faith. My criticism was directed especially toward this text. I sent my report to Rome, and that was all. Cardinal Alfrink did not receive the authorization he requested, but in the meantime the general situation had evolved.

I've narrated the facts in the order in which they came to be known by me, but nothing says that this is their true order. I heard about Cardinal Alfrink's proposal only after Msgr. Wagner's little secret, but it's possible that it actually preceded it. Here's the way things could have happened. Paul VI receives the request of Cardinal Alfrink. The pope thinks it over, seeks counsel, and finally orders the establishment of a special commission. This takes a bit of time. Then the pope wonders whether the solution proposed for Holland wouldn't suit the whole Latin Church, and he calls in Msgr. Wagner. Cardinal Alfrink's proposal, then, was what would have triggered Paul VI's initiative.

Let's return to the work of the commission. When faced with the new mission entrusted to him, Msgr. Wagner's reaction was— as I said—to gather together all the documents. In itself this was a healthy reaction, but it must be admitted that in these circumstances it lacked realism. Putting together such a projected collection would take many years, and people were impatiently awaiting a concrete solution. On the other hand, the documentation was not inacessible to specialists. Msgr. Wagner was then impressed with the urgency of the situation and how, within a short deadline, a real draft must be presented. So, he called for a general meeting. I wasn't a member of his work group, but one day Msgr. Wagner arrived at Louvain to invite me personally. He had also invited Père Bouyer. The meeting, to take place at Locarno, would last one week. I pleaded that I was obligated to teach in Paris on Tuesday and Wednesday. But he insisted, and finally I agreed to go to Locarno for the final days of the week. As usual, I gave my classes in Paris and took the night train from the Gare de Lyon on Wednesday. Thursday morning I arrived in Locarno and went to the address indicated to me. It was a very comfortable Swiss hotel located outside the city, on a hillside, with a splendid view of the lake. I found there a large group of fifteen people, among them Msgr. Wagner, Professor Fischer, Msgr. Schnitzler, Father Jungmann, Père Bouyer, Père Gy, and Dom Vaggagini. They appeared tired, and I understood why. Nothing is so tiring as working as a group, and the larger the group, the more difficult it becomes.

They had reached the point of drafting the three eucharistic prayers. Some options had been adopted. Thus, the prayers had to be of different types. The first would be inspired by the anaphora of Hippolytus in the *Apostolic Tradition*; the second would be of the Gallican type; and the third of the Oriental type. It was also decided to highlight the role of the Holy Spirit in the eucharist. One of the criticisms that could be made of the Roman Canon was precisely that the role of the Holy Spirit was obscured.

Two problems arose in regard to the anaphora of Hippolytus. It didn't contain a *Sanctus* which isn't an original part of the eucharistic prayer. Should this archaic flavor be retained or should the anaphora be made to conform to the other eucharistic prayers? The decision was to insert the *Sanctus*. The other problem was the invocation of the Holy Spirit. The original text of Hippolytus has such an invocation—an epiclesis—after the institution narrative, but it is directed toward the sanctification of the faithful and not the consecration of the bread and wine. So the group decided to add a short consecratory invocation, only they decided it must go before the institution narrative. This resulted in a double epiclesis. The same solution was adopted for the prayer of the Gallican type. But when it came to the Oriental type, they ran into a difficulty. The most logical solution was quite simply to take an authentic Oriental anaphora and translate it into Latin. This is what I proposed, and I suggested taking the Alexandrine Rite anaphora of Saint Basil. My inspiration for this came from one of my students in Paris. During an exam on the Oriental anaphoras I asked him which one he preferred, and without hesitation he replied: "the Alexandrine anaphora of Saint Basil." I asked him why, and he answered that it was the best from a pastoral point of view. In fact, it's the anaphora which explains most clearly and simply the full dispensation of salvation. I made a Latin translation of it, keeping in mind the Roman structure of the clauses, and sent it to Msgr. Wagner. It was favorably received by most of the consultors, but met with strong opposition from a theologian, Dom Vaggagini.

From the eighth century on there was a controversy between the Latins and the Orientals as to the moment of consecration. For the Latins the consecration was effected by the very words of Jesus. For the Orientals it was accomplished by the invocation of the Holy Spirit. This theological controversy never kept Rome from respecting the Oriental tradition. The Orientals who were united to the Church of Rome always kept the epiclesis in its traditional Eastern place, that is, after the institution narrative. The Alexandrine anaphora of Saint Basil was used daily by Catholic Copts. Since Rome accepted this anaphora in Greek and in Coptic, there didn't seem to be any reason why it would not be accepted in Latin. But Dom Vaggagini objected that this would trouble Latin Catholics. Accustomed to considering that the consecration was brought about by the words of Christ, they would not understand that the Holy Spirit still be called upon for the consecration. It wasn't possible to change the place of the epiclesis in this anaphora. What could be done with a newly-composed prayer was impossible with an authentic Oriental anaphora. The majority decided in favor of the anaphora of Saint Basil, but Dom Vaggagini quite honestly let us know that he would argue against this proposal to the Commission. If an authentic Oriental anaphora was not to be adopted, then only one solution remained: compose a text which followed the ordinary outline of the Oriental anaphoras, with the exception of the place of the epiclesis. Dom Vaggagini, taking his inspiration from several anaphoras, had composed a text of this type.

In the presence of the bishops of the Commission there was, in fact, a discussion between Père Bouyer (who defended the anaphora of Saint Basil) and Dom Vaggagini (who rejected it). The result of the vote was fifteen in favor and fourteen against, but the president at that time, Cardinal Confalonieri, considered the majority insufficient, and said that the matter should be referred to the pope. From that moment we had to provide an alternative solution, and the text of Dom Vaggagini, found today in the Roman Missal, was perfected.

I still regret that a genuine anaphora wasn't accepted. From an ecumenical point of view also, it would have been important. It should be noted, besides, that the opposition was not inspired by a spirit of controversy. One bishop, who had been a university professor, declared: "If I were still a professor, I'd have voted in favor, but as a bishop I don't want to create problems." I had argued that, during ecumenical weeks, Oriental Rite priests were invited to celebrate Mass according to their rite in Latin Rite churches. Dom Vagaggini replied that this took place in foreign languages which people didn't understand, and that this couldn't trouble anyone. This is a very debatable point of view, but I didn't have the courage to continue the discussion on this level.

The second stumbling block in the meeting of 1951 was the penitential act. The discussions began again after the Council. The problem was difficult because this was an innovation, and numerous solutions could be found. On the other hand, we had to combine this innovation with the traditional elements of the Roman Mass. I didn't take part in these discussions, and I can't say anything about them. But I do know that some changes were made after the Commission had approved the draft. A few trial runs took place in Rome, and Msgr. Wagner was obliged to introduce some revisions he wasn't satisfied with.

The reform of the Mass covered all the parts of the missal, and there were different work groups. One of them was assigned the task of reforming the prayers and prefaces. In this area the Roman Missal was defective and lacking when compared with the ancient sacramentaries. The number of prefaces proposed was singularly limited, and the prayers were not always well-chosen. It could be enriched by drawing on the treasures of the Roman tradition. The relator of this group was Dom Bruylants. The selection couldn't have been better. His knowledge of the sources of the Latin liturgies was wonderful. He had issued a critical edition of the prayers of the missal and had gathered enormous amounts of information onto file cards. Unfortunately, he was not able to complete his work. It was even said that the work killed him. As I mentioned earlier, he died upon returning home from a meeting of the Commission. After his death Dom Dumas of Hautcombe Abbey assumed his role, and I was asked to become a member of his work group. So I collaborated on the reform of the prayers and prefaces. This was mainly revision work. Dom Dumas used the documentation of his predecessor, and the greater part of the work had been done. Still, I was requested to compose some prayers and prefaces—I'm quite unable to say which ones. These were for the cases in which nothing valid in tradition was found.

17

Confirmation

The Constitution on the Sacred Liturgy wisely called for a revision of confirmation that would show "the intimate connection of this sacrament with the whole of Christian initiation" (par. 70). In spite of this, and on Botte's own admission, "no one dreamed" of having confirmation studied by the post-conciliar work group assigned to baptism.

A diversity of cultural settings and pastoral needs influenced his group's work on revising the rite of confirmation. Botte also explains the reliance of the revised ritual on the Byzantine Rite for the new sacramental formula: "Be sealed with the Gift of the Holy Spirit." How much the deliberations depended on human factors comes through rather clearly. (Tr.)

T HE DISTRIBUTION OF WORK according to the liturgical books assigned confirmation to my group. In fact, this rite was placed in the Pontifical since it was reserved to the bishop. It would have been more logical to have it studied by the group in charge of baptism, but no one dreamed of that.

From a purely liturgical point of view, the ritual of confirmation presented no major problem; but we could have been delayed by theological controversies, and we had to take a stand.

The first question concerned the matter and form of the sacrament. Tradition linked it to the imposition of hands by which the apostles conferred the gift of the Spirit, but, in fact, the rite had evolved. Even in Rome where the imposition of hands existed, it was no longer considered the essential rite: its place had been taken by the anointing with chrism. Some theologians wished that we'd return to the apostolic usage. If in the past the church had the power to change, they said, it still possesses the same power, and nothing need keep the church from doing so again. This reasoning is simple, but it is perhaps a little too simple. If the church has the power, is it appropriate that it be used? At any rate, the answer to this question fell within the competence of the Council strictly speaking, and not of a post-conciliar Commission. Now the Council took care not to make a decision to that effect, and this was not a casual omission since the problem was raised at the pre-conciliar commission. I remember quite well my answer. I remarked that, since this was an ecumenical Council, such a decision would have placed the Orientals in an awkward position. At any rate, this would break the unity existing between the East and the West. I don't know how much weight my intervention might have had, but it's certain the Council didn't want to change anything. In these circumstances it was not up to the Commission to undertake an initiative which would go beyond its competence. Moreover, the imposition of hands was still in the Pontifical, and abolishing it was out of the question. No one insisted on this point.

The other problem was the age of confirmation. This was never a problem in the East where, with confirmation still linked to baptism, chrismation was done by the priest with the myron consecrated by the bishop or the patriarch. In the West, on the contrary, confirmation remained the privilege of the bishop, as successor of the apostles. The outcome was the separation of baptism from confirmation. With the multiplication of country parishes and with the vast area of the provincial dioceses, most baptisms were celebrated without the bishop being present, and confirmation had to be delayed till later on—but this had nothing to do with the age of the candidates. When this problem came up, solutions varied according to place. In fact, there was never a general law in this matter before the promulgation of the *Codex Juris Canonici* in 1917. Even so, it should be noted that a great part of the Latin countries were exempted from this law. The code, indeed, did not abrogate immemorial customs, and Spain, Portugal, and South

America had the custom that children could be confirmed as soon as a competent minister was found.

The legislation of the code was based on Roman jurisprudence and was inspired by a theology. Confirmation is the second phase of Christian initiation, between baptism and eucharist. The practice of delaying confirmation was legitimate, but this delay could not go beyond the age of reason. The drafters of the code patently took their inspiration from Leo XIII, for whom confirmation was a preparation for first communion.

We must admit that the code's promulgation scarcely had an influence on current practice in our area. Quite to the contrary, a movement favoring the delay of confirmation is taking shape. I remember a time when confirmation was presented as the sacrament of Catholic Action. It almost would have been reserved to members of various Catholic youth movements. Today something else is found: confirmation is the sacrament of adolescence. Theory here is based, not on theology, but on psychology. Confirmation has to be delayed till the moment a candidate has reached a degree of maturity that allows one to make a definitive choice and orientation of life. And, it is fitting that this moment be marked by a solemn rite which will be remembered.

Several things are mixed-up here. First of all, one supposes there's a parallelism between a Christian's intellectual development and spiritual growth. By what right can the sacrament of confirmation be declared useless for children, while they can attain sanctity and even be led to give witness to their faith? There have been child martyrs. It's enough to think of the martyrs of Uganda in the last century. Furthermore, there's a mix-up between the efficaciousness of the sacrament and the psychological impact of a great ceremony.

As for the supposed psychology, it looks outdated to me. In our countries adolescence is situated near fourteen years of age. Is this the ideal age for confirmation? Today we have the experience of the Protestants. This was their traditional age. Now they agree that this is the worst age. Some want to advance it by several years, as in the Catholic Church; others hold it off till eighteen. It isn't true, by the way, that fourteen is the age for leaving school and entering real life. The school years have been extended and will be even more so. If you start out from this criterion, you have to agree with that American bishop who set the age for confirmation at eighteen. You arrive at the paradoxical conclusion that people would be mature enough to contract marriage before being ready for confirmation.

The problem was not directly within my competence. Yet it was probable that some members of the Commission would raise it, and I would would be led to take sides. Père Gy wrote me from Rome that an offensive was being prepared in favor of confirmation as a sacrament of adolescence. The Italian bishops had set up a plan of making a joint decision on this matter and submitting it to the pope for approval. The pope was favorable and was prepared to give his approval. This wouldn't be, of course, an infallible decision, but it would be a change since, till then, Roman jurisprudence had been firmly attached to the ancient tradition. To me this seemed regrettable and I decided to react. There was no time to lose. I asked Père Matagne, the director of the *Nouvelle revue théologique*, to insert a short article in the issue which was already at the printer, something he readily granted. It was not a question of a long scholarly article which no one would read, but of taking a position with a clearly polemical tone, one which would start a discussion. The *Nouvelle revue théologique* was altogether suited for this since, having wide circulation, the article wouldn't go unnoticed. The result was immediate. A few days after publication I received at the same time a word of approval from a cardinal in Rome and an insulting letter from a pastor in the Eternal City. This was a good sign. It wasn't long before a series of articles appeared in some Italian journals. To my great surprise, the more important ones went along the same lines as mine: they showed the continuity and consistency of the Roman tradition. The only negative critique I know was an article by Dom Vaggagini in the *Scuola cattolica,* to which I replied in a later issue. The Italian bishops held their meeting but did not make any joint decision; and they didn't make any request of the Holy See. The danger of a definition of confirmation as a sacrament of adolescence was held off for the time being.

Among the commendations I received, the warmest was a letter from Cardinal Duval, the archbishop of Algiers. In thanking him I suggested he write the pope to explain his point of view. It seemed very important to me that the Sovereign Pontiff hear the voice of an experienced pastor. The cardinal wrote the letter. In reply he was told that his letter would be communicated to the competent bodies. I then wrote to the secretariat of the Commission to ask for a copy of the document, but I never received an answer. On the other hand, I was sent a copy of a request from several bishops to the Commission in favor of postponing confirmation until fourteen. It was signed by several bishops from Eastern Europe, behind the Iron Curtain. Here's how they explained the situation. They experienced some difficulty in getting parents to send their children to catechism up till the time the children were fourteen. If confirmation were at this age, the parents would be obliged to send the children to catechism for fear of seeing the sacrament refused. This looked perfectly immoral to me. But since the question was sent by several bishops to the Commission, I was obliged to take sides.

I did so at the next meeting when I presented the two opposing theses. On the one side there was the Roman tradition based on a theology of confirmation: it is the second stage of Christian initiation and cannot be delayed beyond the age of seven since the gift of the Spirit may be needed from the age of reason. On the other side there was a theory based on a debatable psychology which results in some absurd conclusions, such as delaying the sacrament till as late as the age of eighteen. The two theses do not have equal value. The Roman tradition, by its continuity, constitutes a teaching of the church's magisterium. Undoubtedly this tradition is not a matter of papal infallibility, but it cannot be rejected without a very serious reason. Do these reasons exist? And I concluded with two questions: "Can you affirm in your soul and conscience that confirmation is useless to children before fourteen? If this is so, can you assume the responsibility of depriving children of the grace of the sacrament for seven to ten years, especially in dechristianized lands and in those of concealed persecution?" I waited a few seconds, but no one answered "yes" to my two questions. From that point on, the matter was settled. All that those opposed could do was ask for a secret vote, but they couldn't do this without committing themselves, and they didn't dare do so. Anyway, the rest was not in doubt, and they didn't insist.

A result of reserving confirmation to the bishop was a delay in administering this sacrament, but this delay had in turn an influence on the practice of this rite. It became an overwhelming burden for the bishops of far-flung dioceses. It was impossible for the bishop to visit all his parishes every year. The bishop took advantage of his passing through to concentrate in one place the candidates from neighboring parishes, and they were in the hundreds. To spare the bishop's strength, the ceremony had to be a quick one. This occurred in my country not so long ago. Around 1936 I was chaplain in an orphanage, and I had to take the children to sessions of this kind. After saying Mass in the morning I would leave on a bus with my children and those of the village. We were expected by 9:30 at the collegiate church of Huy, but we had to wait before entering till the candidates of the first session came out, since the bishop was working full-time that day. We were in the second group, and there was still a third to come. The bishop proceeded to confirm according to the Roman Pontifical. The editors of this book lacked imagination. They had taken the confirmation section out of the ancient baptismal ritual, but never dreamed of giving it a liturgical setting. There was neither a Mass, nor readings, nor anything that would serve as a preparation. What took time was the children's procession toward the bishop's throne: it was interminable. Of course, there was no community to welcome the children. The citizens of Huy had other things to do, and the children's parents would not take a trip for so little. There were many godfathers and godmothers, but these had only distant connections with the confirmands. Psychologically it was pitiful. It made one think of vaccination sessions.

The first remedy was at least to make a liturgical setting possible. Confirmation would be conferred during a Mass, after the gospel, with the proper parts of the Mass chosen with confirmation in mind. In the event that Mass would not be possible, at least a liturgy of the word could be provided. But this would lengthen the ceremony, whereas some wished it to be brief. To this effect we made two proposals for submission to the pope. The first was to include in the liturgical action the priests who were present: they would share the consignation of the holy chrism with the bishop. The second proposal was to allow the bishops to delegate a priest to confirm in some well-defined cases. Many bishops possessed this faculty, but by virtue of a privilege from the Holy See. What we were asking for was to have this placed in common law. The Commission approved the two proposals.

One imperative reform was that of linking confirmation to baptism. The simplest way was the renewal of the baptismal promises. Here I was surprised to receive a proposal from a South American bishop: add to the traditional promises a promise of fidelity to the Catholic Church. The reason for this was that Catholics were going over to Protestantism. But it makes no sense to promise fidelity to the church after having proclaimed one's faith in the church. My reply was that if I had to propose this to the Commission, I would be bound to state the reason indicated, and this in the presence of the Protestant observers at the sessions. And this would make a painful impression. The bishop didn't insist, and we kept the traditional promises.

The most important reform was that of the sacramental formula. The one in the Pontifical was strongly criticized: it was too long and not very expressive. All were quick to agree that it should be replaced, but then a new one had to be found—not a very easy task. The ancient Roman sources did not contain any extra formulas. Nothing was to stop us from creating a new one, and the group contained a number of people willing to help me. I soon had a whole file of proposals with supporting explanations. My only problem was I had too much to choose from, and it was really too much. It was impossible to submit all these proposals to the Commission. It was all the more difficult to choose since none seemed to be decisive. The weakness of most was that they attempted to say too much. Moreover, I had reservations about proposing a formula that lacked support in tradition. I put the whole file aside and proposed adopting the old formula of the Byzantine Rite, a formula whose foremost quality was its biblical inspiration: "Seal of the gift of the Holy Spirit." The image of a mark, a seal, *sphragis,* to designate the action of the Holy Spirit in Christian initiation comes from Saint Paul in the Epistle to the Ephesians (1:13) in the verbal form of *esphragisthête, signati estis* (you have been sealed). It was widely used by the Fathers of the church. The Byzantine formula, the most ancient of those in use today, is explicitly cited in a document attributed to the Council of Constantinople in 381, but actually dating from 450. With some variants, it's found in other Oriental rites. Thus it has a solid basis in tradition.

The proposal was well received, there being no opposition to it. For a translation I proposed: "Accipe signaculum donationis Sancti Spiritus," but reflection led me to realize that this literal translation could be misunderstood. Modern theology has accustomed us to speaking about the gifts of the Holy Spirit in the plural, and these gifts are something distinct from the Holy Spirit. The same is not true for the language of the Bible which speaks of the gift in the singular. It must be understood as the gift which is the Spirit, who descends, is given, which we receive. The terminology is constant. So I proposed another translation: "Accipe signaculum Spiritus Sancti qui tibi datur" ("Be sealed with the Holy Spirit who is given to you"). This was approved by the Commission.

One final correction was to suppress a rubric introduced very late in the Pontifical. This directive ordered the bishop (at the moment he makes the sign of the cross with his thumb) to place his other four fingers on the head of the candidate. This was not a very natural gesture; it was totally non-expressive. Besides, it was never considered essential. The removal of this rubric, then, wasn't an accidental omission, but an intentional correction approved by the Commission.

Finally, we asked that the rule not allowing the godparent at baptism also to serve as sponsor at confirmation be abolished. This disciplinary measure came from an erroneous interpretation of a canon. On the contrary, it is desirable that, when possible, the same person be the sponsor for the two sacraments.

Several years went by between the time I submitted our draft (duly approved by the Commission) and its promulgation. What occurred during this time? I don't fully know: all I can do is point out some of the corrections made on it.

Our proposal was that the priests present could help the bishop with the anointing, but we reserved to the bishop himself the first laying on of hands. In the published ritual, however, the priests equally share in the imposition of hands. We also had asked that the bishop have the right to delegate a priest to confer confirmation. If we want its dignity restored to the sacrament, we have to avoid confirmation en masse, and give some human dimensions to the ceremony, with a community that welcomes the confirmands and with parents who are present. In these circumstances it would be more and more difficult for the bishop personally to confirm all the candidates. This presents no practical difficulty. All the bishops have or can have an indult from the Holy See granting them this faculty. It seemed desirable that this be put into common law. But it was refused. The bishops must obtain for themselves an indult and pay the fee to Rome. The sacramental formula was also changed. The text approved by the Commission was: "Accipe signaculum Spiritus Sancti qui tibi datur." It now reverted to a more literal translation of the Byzantine formula: "Accipe signaculum doni Spiritus Sancti." But the meaning is not changed. The genitive *Spiritus Sancti* is indeed a genitive of apposition: the gift which is the Holy Spirit.

An apostolic constitution on confirmation precedes the ritual. It is in line with tradition. The gift of the Spirit is indeed the second stage of Christian initiation, not the sacrament of adolescence. I was mistaken in regard to the person who drafted this constitution. Writing a review in *Questions liturgiques et paroissiales*, I thought I recognized the hand of Père Lécuyer in the constitution. A wrong judgment, but not a rash one. In fact, the documentation used in the constitution is identical to what we had gathered together and which is found in our file. Since I wasn't consulted, I thought that Père Lécuyer was asked to handle this task. Upon inquiry, I learned that the text was prepared by Père Dhanis, a Belgian Jesuit at the Gregorian University, and then reviewed by Père Gy.

I can now end my recollections of the liturgical movement. The rite of confirmation, just promulgated this year, is the last document I worked on personally. The rest belongs to the future.

18

Taking Stock

Botte concludes his account by candidly admitting that public opinion was divided on the success of the post-conciliar liturgical reform at the time he completed his book in 1972. He gives a masterful reflection on the historical import of the Catholic Church's shift from Latin back to the vernacular.

Botte then summarizes other themes dear to the proponents of the liturgical movement. To these we might add others as part of an unfinished agenda: for example, adequate musical settings for vernacular texts; liturgical inculturation; new forms and texts of liturgical prayer; the extension of liturgical ministries to more members of the liturgical assembly. (Tr.)

I AM A POOR ACCOUNTANT. I was initiated into this profession in the army during World War I, and I was able to get myself out of this situation only by making mistakes in the books. These have long since been covered by prescription, but I've kept the impression that balance sheets and inventories are always fixed, even when concerned with things as tangible as guns, gas masks, and canned food. Numbers can say just about anything a person wishes when applied to human factors, ideas, and feelings. And so I would not have dreamed of concluding by taking stock unless others had done so before me.

I've followed the liturgical movement for almost sixty years, from its origins till after Vatican II. We all know that the post-conciliar reform has stirred up differing reactions. Alongside the plain people who have accepted it quite simply, there are some thinking people who balk at it. Some complain that we've gone too far and changed our religion; others, feeling we haven't gone far enough, feel they're capable of doing much better. So I feel obligated to give my opinion. I am not under the illusion that everyone will agree, nor do I claim to be pronouncing a definitive judgment. I'll feel happy if I can clear up some confusion and correct some errors.

First of all, justice cannot be done to the liturgical movement by judging it exclusively on the details of the liturgical reform. From the beginning the reform has been a movement of an idea inspired by a certain vision of the mystery of the church and it has exerted a great influence on theology, even outside Catholicism. It is no accident that its founder, Dom Beauduin, became one of the most ardent craftsmen of the ecumenical movement. We must ask whether the movement has remained faithful to its early inspiration. It's the spirit that should be judged, not the letter. To separate one from the other is to resign oneself to understanding nothing.

Another frequent mistake is in the terms of the comparison. What is being compared with what? People wish to compare the old liturgy with the new. What do they mean by the "old"? Do they mean the ideal liturgy, such as can be seen in great abbeys, or rather the one found in most of our parishes? And the new liturgy? Liturgy as prescribed by the Holy See must not be mistaken for the fantasies that can be seen in some places. Those who worked on the liturgical reform are not responsible for the anarchy reigning in some countries, no more than the Council Fathers are responsible for the lack of discipline in some priests. One shouldn't mix everything together.

Let's confine ourselves to the authentic reform. What most shocks some people is the abandonment of Latin. I'm all the more at ease in speaking about this since no one would ever suspect me of being an enemy of Latin. I spent a great part of my life studying and interpreting old texts. I don't feel any personal joy in celebrating the liturgy with texts that aren't always excellent, whether in French or Dutch. I remain attached to Gregorian Chant, and I'm happy that we've partially retained it at Mont César. Admittedly, abandoning Latin can be a cause of impoverishment—not only from the esthetic but also from the real content point of view. If I had followed my own tastes and personal preferences, I would have defended Latin in the face of all opposition. Still, I became an advocate of the vernacular because in conscience I deemed it necessary for the well-being of the church. In conscience I judged it more worthwhile to sacrifice the letter in order to be faithful to the spirit.

From the beginning the liturgical movement's goal was to create living assemblies and communities who participate to the fullest in the prayer and life of the church. To overcome the barrier of Latin, translations were made, with some positive results in countries with longstanding cultures. But after fifty year's experience can we affirm that this was the ideal as far as the universal church was concerned. An ecumenical council was the occasion for raising the question. Present were bishops from around the world, in particular from mission countries. They should be the ones to ask in order to find out whether maintaining Latin was a handicap for the young churches of Africa and Asia. If this were done, then there would be no possible hesitation since evangelization comes first.

Besides, even in Europe many were hoping for a greater use of the vernacular, especially in de-christianized regions. Classical culture was in clear decline, and many priests had no more than a rudimentary knowledge of Latin. I can say this because I am fully acquainted with the facts. Just reread what I said earlier in connection with the Paris Institut de Liturgie. Also, Roman jurisprudence had become more flexible. Rome had conceded some vernacular lectionaries and bilingual rituals. The door was ajar. Should it be opened all the way or suddenly reclosed? The Council came out in favor of opening it further, and we must now move ahead.

This raises many problems which can't be perfectly resolved in one day, in particular, the question of translations and liturgical music. It's evident that the improvised creations we experience are often rather poor esthetically. We must try to do better, and there's room for interesting research. While we wait, this is no reason for closing our eyes to the positive aspects of the reform.

The goal of the liturgical movement has been to get the Christian people to participate in the prayer of the church in the most active and conscious manner possible. Has this goal been reached? Right off I would reply "yes." I've attended Masses in parishes in Belgium, France, and Italy. These were ordinary parishes where the reform was carried out without any eccentricity. There were no silent spectators: everyone responded, everyone listened. These were really communities of people praying together, so completely different from the Masses I knew in my childhood when each person kept busy as best one could or just waited for the Mass to be over. I don't think that high school students, already accustomed to the new liturgy, could bear what was inflicted on us sixty years ago. The assemblies I'm referring to were also assemblies with many communicants and thus had recovered the true sense of the eucharist. Here all participated in the Lord's sacrifice. Throughout my whole youth there was a sort of divorce between the Mass and communion. People went to communion before Mass or after Mass, sometimes in the middle of Mass, but never at the same time as the priest. Communion was an act of private devotion with people seeking to be alone with the Lord, but this has nothing to do with the Mass. It was no longer an action of the community which brought all Christians together at the one meal of the Lord. Leading Christians back to receiving communion together is an important achievement of the liturgical movement.

Another positive outcome is the enrichment of the liturgy of the word. Not only are Christians able to hear the proclamation of the word of God in their own language, but attempts have been made to increase and vary the readings so that, at the end of three years, the faithful can hear the essential passages of the Bible, including the Hebrew Scriptures. This has been subjected to the most surprising criticism. Although some have seen in this a harmful influence of Protestantism, it is a return to the most ancient and universal tradition. The homilies of the ancient Church Fathers, both Greek and Latin, testify to it, since the Scripture was the basis of preaching. And the Council expressly indicated its desire for a return to biblical preaching.

The reform of the Mass has been accomplished in the spirit of tradition. I have already spoken of this earlier, but I believe it should be stressed here. This is not the work of leftists ignorant of tradition. What is most striking are the changes in the rites of the offering. The best liturgists were agreed on simplifying this part. As level-headed a man as Dom Capelle was of the same mind as Father Jungmann. The offertory prayers were extraneous to the authentic Roman tradition: not only were they unknown to Saint Gregory but they weren't even found in the copy of the sacramentary sent by Pope Hadrian to Charlemagne. These were the devotional prayers of the priest, prayers which had infiltrated the Roman-Germanic use. Their drawback was to grant this rite exaggerated importance to the detriment of the true offering which traditionally was made after the institution narrative. In all rites the true offering is not the bread and wine as material gifts, but the body and blood of Christ under the forms of bread and wine. The accent was shifted by this development of the offertory prayers. There was a time in the liturgical movement when the offering of these gifts looked to some like the culminating point of the Mass, and when offertory processions were organized with all kinds of offerings. This was a deviation needing correction.

The eucharistic prayers also remain in conformity with the spirit of tradition. The old canon of Saint Gregory underwent only some slight retouches. The new formulas are inspired by authentic texts of the ancient liturgies. The first, recapturing the most ancient eucharistic prayer known to us, was composed at Rome in the third century in Greek, and for centuries it has been said by priests of the Ethiopian Rite. It doesn't mar the Roman Missal which has taken it in.

A comparison between the new edition of the Roman Missal with the former edition shows the presence of a great many new pieces, prayers and prefaces. This isn't an innovation: the treasures of the ancient Roman sacramentaries were searched to enrich today's liturgy, but the edition is too recent to have had time to make vernacular translations.

The reform that pleases me the most is the return to concelebration. Priests living in a community found it impossible to receive communion together. Each had to celebrate Mass in private, and then all could come together to attend a Mass at which no one went to communion. Thus there was a series of Masses which ensued at a fast clip at the side altars and which did not always edify the people. It appeared that the multiplication of private Masses was an end in itself. But to crown it all off, there were days when each priest was allowed to say three Masses. This was a veritable marathon. I remember Christmas days when, after attending Mass at night without going to communion, we felt obliged to get in three low Masses while waiting for the daytime Mass, which we attended without receiving communion. There was something abnormal with that.

As far as essentials are concerned, the reform has always remained faithful to the spirit of the liturgical movement. The reform, although the result of the liturgical movement, is above all else a starting point. It is a plan for the future, and it would be a risky illusion to expect immediate, spectacular results from it.

Such an illusion presupposes a rather simplistic idea of liturgical reform, one which views the reform as a set of recipes destined to make the Mass more attractive and to fill the churches which were beginning to empty. This is to commit oneself to a dangerous pragmatism whose only criterion is success. Everything is good which attracts crowds. This leads to an escalation of undertakings which go from a touching naiveté to the eccentric.

True liturgical reform has nothing do to with this sort of display. First of all, the reform cannot be separated from the doctrinal work of the Council since the liturgy must express in worship the faith of the church. During the Council the Fathers of Vatican II reflected on the question of the church because it is the theological problem of the twentieth century, not only in Catholicism but in all Christian confessions. It is in the church that the plan of God for bringing us all together in Christ is to be accomplished. The Council Fathers returned to the sources of Revelation and made a distinction between human routine and the authentic tradition which ensures continuity in the life of the church. The Council's desire was that this renewed faith in the church be expressed in the liturgy so that the liturgy permeate the whole life of individuals and communities.

The will of the Council is affirmed in more than one place in the Constitution on the Liturgy. This is why the document asks that the word of God be widely proclaimed in the language of the people. This is why it recommends that the true nature and simplicity of the rites be made evident. The Council Fathers wanted a rather flexible reform, one allowing to the episcopal conferences a certain amount of freedom for adaptation. But the Fathers of Vatican II especially insisted on a renewal of catechesis and preaching.

This isn't the place to critique the state of preaching in the Catholic Church. A whole literature exists on the subject, and there is general agreement that it is poor. Sunday preaching, in particular, became a parenthetical element during which matters having no connection with the assembly were mentioned. I recall an outline for preaching on social questions, according to which the sermon for the fourth Sunday after Easter was about Christian labor unions. Moreover, many priests showed a certain loss of affection for preaching. As for the faithful, it didn't bother them to arrive after the sermon, or else they used this time to go to the café across from the church to drink a cup of coffee. There was a lack of balance in the Sunday assembly, an imbalance the Council wanted to correct by insisting on the importance of preaching. Preaching has always been an essential element of the Sunday assembly. Christians have the right not only to take part in the Lord's Supper but also to receive the bread of the word of God to nourish their faith and piety. Now, the word of God is not solely the reading of the Bible, but also the commentary on the reading by the assembly's presider. This is the most ancient and most authentic tradition to which the Council wants to return. The intent of the Council would not be attained by juxtaposing a lecture on just any topic with a eucharistic celebration. By restoring balance to the assembly the Council also wanted to return its cohesion and unity. Preaching, always to be at the service of the liturgy, has as its goal helping each one of the faithful to assimilate the teaching of the Scriptures and to form the assembly into a community of faith and prayer. The fact that the liturgy is celebrated in the vernacular doesn't make the sermon superfluous—quite the contrary. According to the Council's wish, the selection of readings has been enriched, especially for the Hebrew Scriptures. Since Catholics lack a biblical formation, a commentary is all the more necessary.

I have arrived at the end of my project. I have given witness to and gathered my recollections of the liturgical movement, from its origins till this winter of 1972. My goal was to show what the movement was and how it led to the post-conciliar reform. It was also my desire that the spirit of this reform be better understood by those who have to implement it. You might ask what the impact of this reform will be on the life of the church. I am not a prophet nor a clairvoyant, and I won't dare make any long-range predictions. Besides, I imagine that the outcome will not be the same everywhere. It will vary according to the fidelity of those responsible—priests and bishops—to the spirit and teaching of the Council.

As far as I'm concerned, I remain optimistic because I never had any illusions. I never expected any sensational results. It is a dangerous illusion to believe that the church would abruptly change, and thereafter become a community of saints. It's enough to reread the parable of the weeds to be convinced of this, but there's another parable that gives confidence, namely, that of the sower. I believe in the power of God's word. When it doesn't encounter obstacles, it grows irresistibly and produces a hundredfold. There is much good earth which is eager to open itself to the sowing of God's word, but we must provide this word. This is the request of the Council: preaching inspired by the word of God which clarifies and nourishes the faith of the people. In my opinion this is the most serious problem of the liturgical reform. The rest is secondary. I hope that those responsible would become more and more aware of this.

Nevertheless, I remain optimistic because, above all else, I have faith in the church. I just began my eightieth year. On 14 June I celebrated the fiftieth anniversary of my priestly ordination. I give thanks to God for having been able to serve Christ and the church for so long a time. They are inseparable to me. In spite of the scandals and abuses the church of Christ is the guardian of the deposit of faith. It's the church of the apostles, of the martyrs, and of the saints of all times. During the Council the Holy Spirit visibly inspired in the church the desire to purify itself and to return to its ideal. We should believe that the Spirit is still there, according to Christ's promise, and that he will complete the work he began.

Bibliography of Bernard Botte

This bibliography, compiled by Françoise Petit and which appeared in *Mélanges liturgiques offerts au R.P. dom Bernard Botte O.S.B.* (Louvain, 1972) and was updated in *Questions liturgiques* (61:2/3, 1980) omits the book summaries and notices signed by Dom Botte. Nevertheless, these constitute no small part of his scholarly activity, for they probably number in the thousands.

The majority of these are found in *Recherches de théologie ancienne et médiévale* and especially in its complementary series, the *Bulletin de théologie ancienne et médiévale* (Louvain, Mont César, since 1929). Dom Botte collaborated here from their beginnings. First he was responsible for presenting studies relative to the history of exegesis; then, since 1948, he undertook analyses of publications on patristics for the first four centuries.

Since 1932 he contributed regularly to the oldest publication of Mont César, *Les questions liturgiques et paroissiales* which since 1970 appears under the abbreviated title of *Questions liturgiques*.

Dom Botte occasionally contributed notices to the following reviews:

Bulletin d'ancienne littérature latine chrétienne (Maredsous),
Revue d'histoire ecclésiastique (University of Louvain),
Vigiliae christianae (Nijmegen).

The numbers in parentheses indicate reeditions or translations that do not modify the original version.

1. Deus meus, Deus meus, ut quid dereliquisti me?, *Les questions liturgiques et paroissiales*, 11, 1926, 105-114.
2. La gloire du Christ dans l'evangile de saint Jean, *Les questions liturgiques et paroissiales*, 12, 1927, 65-76.
3. Jean le théologien, *Divus Thomas, Commentarium de philosophia et theologia* (Piacenza), 30, 1927, 382-388.
4. L'invocation du Christ dans l'avant-messe, *Cours et conférences des semaines liturgiques*, 6, 1928, 105-117.
5. L'ange du sacrifice, *Cours et conférences des semaines liturgiques*, 7, 1929, 209-221.
6. L'ange du sacrifice et l'épiclèse de la messe romaine au moyen âge, *Recherches de théologie ancienne et médiévale*, 1, 1929, 285-308.
7. La Sagesse dans les Livres sapientiaux, *Revue des sciences philosophiques et théologiques*, 19, 1930, 83-94.
8. Les origines de l'eucharistie, sacrement et sacrifice, *Les questions liturgiques et paroissiales*, 16, 1931, 171-178.
9. La Sagesse et les origines de la christologie, *Revue des sciences philosophiques et théologiques*, 21, 1932, 54-67.
10. *Les origines de la Noël et de l'Épiphanie. Étude historique* (Coll.: Textes et études liturgiques, 1), Louvain, Mont César, 1932. [See no. 147.]
11. Les évangiles du temps de Nöel, *Les questions liturgiques et paroissiales*, 17, 1932, 294-299.
12. La première fête mariale de la liturgie romaine, *Ephemerides liturgicae*, 47 (N.S. 7), 1933, 425-430. [See no. 16.]
13. *Grammaire grecque du Nouveau Testament*, Paris, J. de Gigord, 1933.
14. L'idée du sacerdoce des fidèles dans la tradition. I: L'antiquité chrétienne, in *Cours et conférences des semaines liturgiques*, 11, 1934, 21-28. Also published in a separate fascicle entitled *Le sacerdoce des fidèles*, collecting the studies of B. Botte, A. Charlier, A. Robeyns and B. Capelle (with an error on the title page; read: T.XI and not T.X), 3-10.
15. *Le canon de la messe romaine. Édition critique, introduction et notes* (Coll.: Textes et études liturgiques, 2), Louvain, Mont César, 1935.
16. G. BERAN and B. BOTTE, A proposito della prima festa mariale della liturgia romana, *Ephemerides liturgicae*, 49 (N.S. 9), 1935, 261-264. [See no. 12.]
17. Secundi meriti munus, *Les questions liturgiques et paroissiales*, 21, 1936, 84-88.
18. Consummare, *Archivum latinitatis medii aevi (Bulletin Du Cange)*, 12, 1937, 43-45.
19. L'apôtre saint Paul et le culte chrétien, *Les questions liturgiques et paroissiales*, 22, 1937, 93-99.
20. *Evangile selon saint Luc. Texte établi et annoté* (Coll.: Classiques grecs), Paris, J. de Gigord, 1937. [See no. 28.]
21. Art. Ferrar (Groupe de manuscrits de), *Dictionnaire de la Bible, Supplément*, 3, 1938, 272-274.
22. Art. Freer (Logion de), *Dictionnaire de la Bible, Supplément*, 3, 1938, 525-527.
23. Art. Freer (Manuscrits de la collection), *Dictionnaire de la Bible, Supplément*, 3, 1938, 527-530.

24. Art. Freising (Fragments de), *Dictionnaire de la Bible, Supplément*, 3, 1938, 530-532.

25. La XXe semaine liturgique française du Mont César (1-4 août 1938), *Les questions liturgiques et paroissiales*, 23, 1938, 225-228.

26. L'ordination de lecteur dans le Pontifical romain, *Les questions liturgiques et paroissiales*, 24, 1939, 36-37.

27. Le rituel d'ordination des Statuta Ecclesiae antiqua, *Recherches de théologie ancienne et médiévale*, 11, 1939, 223-241.

28. *Évangile selon saint Luc. Texte établi et annoté.* Deuxième édition revue (Coll.: Classiques grecs), Paris, J. de Gigord, 1939. [See no. 20.]

29. Le sacre épiscopal dans le rite romain, *Les questions liturgiques et paroissiales*, 25, 1940, 22-32.

30. La scansion des hymnes de l'office, *Les questions liturgiques et paroissiales*, 25, 1940, 151-162.

31. Confessor, *Archivum latinitatis medii aevi (Bulletin Du Cange)*, 16, 1941, 137-148.

32. Imitatio, *Archivum latinitatis medii aevi (Bulletin Du Cange)*, 16, 1941, 149-154.

33. *Le Nouveau Testament. Traduction nouvelle d'après le texte grec*, Turnhout, Brepols, 1944.

34. Le nouveau psautier du Bréviaire romain, *La revue nouvelle*, 1, 1945, 355-360.

35. Noël, fête de lumière, *La revue nouvelle*, 1, 1945, 517-521.

36. *Hippolyte de Rome. La tradition apostolique. Texte latin, introduction, traduction et notes* (Coll.: Sources chrétiennes, 11), Paris, Éditions du Cerf, 1946. [See no. 167.]

37. Paschalibus initiata mysteriis, *Ephemerides liturgicae*, 61 (N.S. 21), 1947, 77-87.

38. L'épiclèse de l'anaphore d'Hippolyte, *Recherches de théologie ancienne et médiévale*, 14, 1947, 241-251.

39. Conficere corpus Christi, *L'année théologique*, 8, 1947, 309-315.

40. Prima resurrectio. Un vestige de millénarisme dans les liturgies occidentales, *Recherches de théologie ancienne et médiévale*, 15, 1948, 5-17.

41. L'onction des malades, *La Maison-Dieu*, no. 15, 1948, 91-107.

42. La Constitution apostolique Sacramentum ordinis, *La Maison-Dieu*, no. 16, 1948, 124-129.

43. Processionis aditus, *Miscellanea liturgica in honorem L. Cuniberti Mohlberg*, I (Bibliotheca Ephemerides liturgicae, 22), Rome, 1948, 127-133.

44. Art. Itala, *Dictionnaire de la Bible, Supplément*, 4, 1949, 777-782.

45. Le lectionnaire arménien et la fête de la Théotocos à Jérusalem au Ve siècle, *Sacris erudiri*, 2, 1949, 111-122.

46. L'authenticité de la Tradition apostolique de saint Hippolyte, *Recherches de théologie ancienne et médiévale*, 16, 1949, 177-185.

47. L'anaphore chaldéenne des apôtres, *Orientalia christiana periodica*, 15, 1949, 259-276.

48. Liturgie chrétienne et liturgie juive, *Cahiers sioniens*, 3, 1949, 215-223.

49. *Ambroise de Milan. Des sacrements. Des mystères. Texte établi, traduit et annoté* (Coll.: Sources chrétiennes, 25), Paris, Éditions du Cerf, 1950. [See no. 133.]

50. A propos de la réforme du Bréviaire, *Les questions liturgiques et paroissiales*, 31, 1950, 1-4.

51. Le culte des saints de l'Ancien Testament dans l'Église chrétienne, *Cahiers sioniens*, 4, 1950, 38-47.

52. Une fête du prophète Élie en Gaule au VIe siècle, *Cahiers sioniens*, 4, 1950, 170-177.

53. La prière du célébrant, *La Maison-Dieu*, no. 20, 1950, 133-152.

(54). Principes de traduction, *La Maison-Dieu*, no. 23, 1950, 31-36. [See nos. 75 and 155.]

(55). Excursus sur deux points obscurs du canon de la messe: Rationabilem, In unitate Spiritus Sancti, *La Maison-Dieu*, no. 23, 1950, 47-53. [See no. 75.]

56. Art. Apertio aurium, *Reallexikon für Antike und Christentum*, 1, 1950, 487-489.

57. Art. Archiereus, *Reallexikon für Antike und Christentum*, 1, 1950, 602-604.

58. Abraham dans la liturgie, *Cahiers sioniens*, 5, 1951, 88-95.

59. Une réunion liturgique internationale à l'abbaye de Maria Laach (12-15 juillet 1951), *Les questions liturgiques et paroissiales*, 32, 1951, 221-223. [See no. 61.]

60. Die früheren Reformen des römischen Breviers, *Anima* (Olten), 6, 1951, 260-269.

(61). Die internationalen liturgischen Studientage in der Abtei Maria Laach, *Anima* (Olten), 6, 1951, 354-358. [Translation of no. 59]

62. Décret de la Congrégation des rites sur les ordinations, *La Maison-Dieu*, no. 25, 1951, 134-139.

63. Note sur l'auteur du De universo attribué à saint Hippolyte, *Recherches de théologie ancienne et médiévale*, 18, 1951, 5-18.

64. Note sur le symbole baptismal de saint Hippolyte, *Mélanges Joseph de Ghellinck, S.J.* (Coll.: Museum Lessianum, Section historique, 13), Gembloux, 1951, I, 189-200.

65. Sitivit anima mea ad Deum fontem vivum (Ps. 41, 3), *Recherches de théologie ancienne et médiévale*, 19, 1952, 17-25.

66. Nuit pascale et chant de communion, *La Maison-Dieu*, no. 29, 1952, 101-106.

67. Le cycle liturgique et l'économie du salut, *La Maison-Dieu*, no. 30, 1952, 63-78.

68. Cycle liturgique et célébrations humaines, *La Maison-Dieu*, no. 30, 1952, 79-82.

69. A propos de virgules. (La ponctuation de la préface), *La Maison-Dieu*, no. 30, 1952, 156-160.

70. La bénédiction du cierge pascal et le cierge des fidèles, *La Maison-Dieu*, no. 31, 1952, 140-143.

71. L'interprétation des textes baptismaux, *La Maison-Dieu*, no. 32, 1952, 18-39.

72. Le choix des lectures de la veillée pascale, *Les questions liturgiques et paroissiales*, 33, 1952, 65-70.

73. A propos des manuels de liturgie, *Les questions liturgiques et paroissiales*, 33, 1952, 117-124.

74. Antiphona, *Sacris erudiri*, 4, 1952, 239-244.

75. B. BOTTE and Chr. MOHRMANN, *L'ordinaire de la messe. Texte critique, traduction et études* (Coll.: Études liturgiques, 2), Paris, Éditions du Cerf et Louvain, Mont César, 1953. Histoire des prières de l'ordinaire de la messe, 15-27. Principes de la traduction, 49-54 [See nos. 54 and 155.] Amen, 97-104. Maiestas, 111-113. Rationabilis, 117-122. In unitate Spiritus Sancti, 133-139. [See no. 55.] Pietas, 141-143. Ite missa est, 145-149.

76. L'oeuvre liturgique de dom Bernard Capelle, *Les questions liturgiques et paroissiales*, 34, 1953, 53-56.

77. Les rapports du baptisé avec la communauté chrétienne, *Les questions liturgiques et paroissiales*, 34, 1953, 115-126.

78. Note historique sur la concélébration dans l'Église ancienne, *La Maison-Dieu*, no. 35, 1953, 9-23.

79. Le "Saint Pierre" d'Oscar Cullman. Notes exégétiques, *Irénikon*, 26, 1953, 140-145.

80. A. BAUMSTARK, *Liturgie comparée. Principes et méthodes pour l'étude historique des liturgies chrétiennes. Troisième édition revue par dom Bernard Botte* (Coll.: Irénikon), Chevetogne, Éditions du Chevetogne, 1953. [See no. 114.]

81. Problèmes de l'anamnèse, *The Journal of Ecclesiastical History*, 5, 1954, 16-24. [A lecture given in Paris, Saint-Serge, 1953.]

(82). L'ordre d'après les prières d'ordination, *Les questions liturgiques et paroissiales*, 35, 1954, 167-179. [Without notes; see no. 110.]

83. Art. Canon missae, *Reallexikon für Antike und Christentum*, 2, 1954, 842-845.

84. L'épiclèse dans les liturgies syriennes orientales, *Sacris erudiri*, 6, 1954, 48-72.

85. Notes de critique textuelle sur l'Adversus haereses de saint Irénée, *Recherches de théologie ancienne et médiévale*, 21, 1954, 165-178.

86. Le problème synoptique, *Bible et vie chrétienne*, no. 7, 1954, 116-122.

87. La Vie de Moïse par Philon, *Cahiers sioniens*, 8, 1954 (special issue), 173-180. Reprinted in the collection: *Moïse, l'homme de l'Alliance*, Tournai and Paris, Desclée et Cie, 1955, 55-62.

88. Un nouveau dictionnaire du latin des chrétiens, *Revue bénédictine*, 65, 1955, 166-270.

89. Le texte de la Tradition apostolique, *Recherches de théologie ancienne et médiévale*, 22, 1955, 161-172.

90. La question pascale: Pâque du vendredi ou Pâque du dimanche?, *La Maison-Dieu*, no. 41, 1955, 84-95.

91. Le culte du prophète Élie dans l'Église chrétienne, in the collection: *Élie le prophète. I: Selon les Écritures et les Traditions chrétiennes* (Coll.: Les études carmélitaines), Paris, Desclée De Brouwer, 1956, 208-218.

92. Presbyterium et Ordo episcoporum, *Irénikon*, 29, 1956, 5-27. [Reprinted with a different title in no. 111.]

93. Le baptême dans l'Église syrienne, *L'Orient syrien*, 1, 1956, 137-155.

94. Note sur la signation d'un enfant, *L'Orient syrien*, 1, 1956, 185-188.

95. Saint Irénée et l'Épître de Clément, *Mémorial Gustave Bardy, Revue des études augustiniennes*, 2, 1956, 67-70.

96. Le nouvel Institut supérieur de liturgie de Paris, *Les questions liturgiques et paroissiales*, 37, 1956, 132-133.

97. L'origine des Canons d'Hippolyte, *Mélanges Mgr Michel Andrieu, Revue des sciences religieuses* (special issue), Strasbourg, 1956, 53-63.

98. Art. Koridethi (Évangiles de), *Dictionnaire de la Bible, Supplément*, 5, 1957, 192-196.

99. Art. Latines (Versions) antérieurs à S. Jérôme, *Dictionnaire de la Bible, Supplément*, 5, 1957, 334-347.

100. Art. Manuscrits grecs du Nouveau Testament, *Dictionnaire de la Bible, Supplément*, 5, 1957, 819-835.

101. Art. Melphictensis (Codex), *Dictionnaire de la Bible, Supplément*, 5, 1957, 1101-1102.

102. Un témoin du texte césaréen du quatrième évangile: 1 253, *Mélanges bibliques rédigés en l'honneur de André Robert*, Paris, Bloud et Gay, (1957), 466-469.

103. Histoire et théologie. A propos du problème de l'Église, *Istina*, 4, 1957, 389-400.

104. Les dimanches de la dédicace dans les Églises syriennes, *L'Orient syrien*, 2, 1957, 65-70.

105. La formule d'ordination "La grace divine" dans les rites orientaux, *L'Orient syrien*, 2, 1957, 285-296.

106. A propos de l'Adversus haereses III.3.2. de saint Irénée, *Irénikon*, 30, 1957, 156-163.

107. Communicantes, *Les questions liturgiques et paroissiales*, 38, 1957, 119-123.

108. L'Institut supérieur de liturgie de Paris, *Les questions liturgiques et paroissiales*, 38, 1957, 123-125.

109. Missels et traductions bibliques. (A propos de missels récents), *Bible et vie chrétienne*, no. 16, 1957, 104-113.

110. L'ordre d'après les prières d'ordination, in the collection: *Études sur le sacrement de l'Ordre* (Coll: Lex orandi, 22), Paris: Éditions du Cerf, 1957, 13-35. [Reproduces no. 82, with notes.] [See no. 134.]

(111). Caractère collégial du presbyterat et de l'episcopat, in the collection: *Études sur le sacrement de l'Ordre* (Coll.: Lex orandi, 22), Paris, Éditions du Cerf, 1957, 97-124. [Reproduces no. 92.] [See no. 135.]

112. Les saints de l'Ancien Testament, *La Maison-Dieu*, no. 52, 1957, 109-120.

113. Art. Competentes, *Reallexikon für Antike und Christentum, III*, 1957, 266-268.

(114). *Comparative Liturgy by Anton Baumstark, revised by Bernard Botte, O.S.B.* English Edition by F.L. Cross, London, A.R. Mowbray, 1958. [Translation of no. 80.]

115. Les anciennes versions de la Bible, *La Maison-Dieu*, no. 53, 1958, 89-109.

116. Le vocabulaire ancien de la confirmation, *La Maison-Dieu*, no. 54, 1958, 89-109.

117. *ΨΕΛΛΙΣΤΗΣ-ΨΑΛΙΣΤΗΣ*, *Mélanges Sévérien Salaville, Revue des études byzantines*, 16, 1958, 162-165.

118. Le texte du Quatrième Évangile et le Papyrus Bodmer II, *Bible et vie chrétienne*, no. 24, 1958, 96-107.

119. La semaine d'études liturgiques de Saint-Serge: baptême et confirmation (Paris, 1-5 juillet 1958), *Les questions liturgiques et paroissiales*, 39, 1958, 235-237.

120. A propos des répons de l'office, *Les questions liturgiques et paroissiales*, 40, 1959, 139-142.

121. La semaine d'études liturgiques de Saint-Serge: les ordinations (Paris, 29 juin - 2 juillet 1959), *Les questions liturgiques et paroissiales*, 40, 1959, 311-312.

122. C. MUNIER, *Les Statuta ecclesiae antiqua. Édition. Études critiques*, Paris, Presses Universitaires de France, 1960. Preface by Dom Botte.

123. Art. Orientales de la Bible (Versions), *Dictionnaire de la Bible, Supplément*, 6, 1960. I: Versions arabes, 807-810. III: Versions coptes, 818-825. IV: Versions éthiopiennes, 825-829.

124. Art. Papyrus bibliques, *Dictionnaire de la Bible, Supplément*, 6, 1960, 1109-1120.

125. Les plus anciennes collections canoniques, *L'Orient syrien*, 5, 1960, 331-350.

126. Un passage difficile de la Tradition apostolique sur le signe de croix, *Recherches de théologie ancienne et médiévale*, 27, 1960, 5-19.

127. La collégialité dans le Nouveau Testament et chez les Pères apostoliques, in the collection: *Le concile et les conciles. Contribution à l'histoire de la vie conciliaire de l'Église* (Coll.: Unam sanctam. Special volume), Chevetogne, Éditions de Chevetogne and Paris, Éditions du Cerf, 1960, 1-18. [See no. 136.]

128. Fragments d'une anaphore inconnue attribuée à S. Épiphane, *Le Muséon*, 73, 1960, 311-315.

129. La semaine d'études liturgiques de Saint-Serge: Pâques (Paris, 4-7 juillet 1960), *Les questions liturgiques et paroissiales*, 41, 1960, 374-375. [See no. 146.]

130. A.-G. MARTIMORT, *L'Église en prière*, Tournai et Paris, Desclée et Cie, 1961[1], 1962[2]. A collective volume: Dom Botte signed the following pages: Introduction générale. II: Rites et familles liturgiques, 15-33. Esquisse d'une histoire de la liturgie. #1: Des origines au concile de Trente, 34-43. [See no. 158.] The 1961 edition was translated into several languages: *La Chiesa in preghiera*, Rome, Desclée et Cie, 1963. See 16-36 and 37-47.
Handbuch der Liturgiewissenschaft, Fribourg, Herder, 1963, 2 vol. See I, 16-35 and 37-46.
La Iglesia en oración (Coll.: Biblioteca Herder, Sección de Liturgia, 58), Barcelona, Herder, 1964. See 45-63 and 64-73.
Handbuch der Liturgiewissenchaft, Leipzig, St. Benno-Verlag, 1965, 2 vol. See I, 16-35 and 37-46.

131. A propos de la formation liturgique dans les séminaires, *La Maison-Dieu*, no. 66, 1961, 70-76.

132. A propos de la réform du psautier latin, *Revue bénédictine*, 71, 1961, 366-371.

133. *Ambroise de Milan, Des sacrements. Des mystères. Explication du Symbole. Texte établi, traduit et annoté.* Nouvelle édition revue et augmentée (Coll.: Sources chrétiennes, 25 bis), Paris, Éditions du Cerf, 1961. [See no. 49.]

(134). Holy Orders in the Ordination Prayers, in the collection: *The Sacrament of Holy Orders,* Collegeville, The Liturgical Press, 1962, 5-23. [Translation of no. 110.]

(135). Collegiate Character of the Presbyterate and Episcopate, in the collection: *The Sacrament of Holy Orders,* Collegeville, The Liturgical Press, 1962, 75-97. [Translation of no. 111.]

(136). Die Kollegialität im Neuen Testament und bie den apostolischen Vätern, in the collection: *Das Konzil und die Konzile,* Stuttgart, Schwabenverlag, 1962, 1-21. [Translation of no. 127.]

137. La traduction des textes du rituel baptismal, *La Maison-Dieu,* no. 71, 1962, 62-68.

138. Notes sur l'Évangéliaire de Rabbula, *Revue des Sciences religieuses,* 36, 1962, 13-26.

139. Sacramentum catechumenorum, *Les questions liturgiques et paroissiales,* 43, 1962, 322-330.

140. O. CASEL, *La fête de Pâques dans l'Église des Pères* (Coll.: Lex orandi, 37), Paris, Éditions du Cerf, 1963. [French translation by J.C. Didier from the original German edition: Art und Sinn der älteste Christlichen Ostfeier, *Jahbuch für Liturgiewissenschaft,* 14, 1934, 1-78. Republished separately under the same title, Münster/Westf., Aschendorff, 1938]. Preface by Dom Botte, 7-10.

141. Le concile et la liturgie, *Revue générale belge,* 99, 1963, 41-48.

142. Le problème de l'adaptation en liturgie, *Revue du clergé africain,* 18, 1963, 307-330. [See nos. 148 and 203.]

143. Les heures de prière dans la Tradition apostolique et les documents derivées, in the collection: *La prière des heures* (Coll.: Lex orandi, 35), Paris, Éditions du Cerf, 1963, 101-115. [A lecture given in Paris, Saint-Serge, 1961.] See also the introduction, 9-13.

144. *La Tradition apostolique de saint Hippolyte. Essai de reconstitution* (Coll.: Liturgiewissenschaftliche Quellen und Forschungen, 39), Münster/Westf., Aschendorff, 1963. [The 2nd and 3rd printings are without changes. For the 4th printing see no. 192.]

145. La sputation, antique rite baptismal?, *Mélanges offerts à Mademoiselle Christine Mohrmann,* Utrecht et Anvers, Spectrum, 1963, 196-201.

146. Pascha, *L'Orient syrien,* 8, 1963, 213-226. [A lecture given in Paris, Saint-Serge, 1960; see no. 129.]

(147). *Los orígenes de la Navidad y de la Epifanía.* Translated from the French by F. PÉREZ (Coll.: El futuro de la verdad), Madrid, Editorial Taurus, 1964. [See no. 10.]

(148). The Problem of Liturgical Adaptation, *African Ecclesiastical Review,* 6, 1964, 3-15 and 126-137. [Translation of no. 142.]

149. L'Euchologe de Sérapion est-il authentique?, *Oriens christianus,* 48, 1964, 50-56.

150. A propos de la Constitution du concile sur la liturgie, *Église vivante,* 16, 1964, 83-90.

151. Art. Hippolytus (Canons of), *Encyclopedia Britannica*, 11, 1964, 520.

152. A propos du caractère collégial du presbytérat et de l'épiscopat, *Concilium*, no. 4, 1965, 161-165.

153. Le problème des ordres mineurs, *Les questions liturgiques et paroissiales*, 46, 1965, 26-31.

154. Dominus vobiscum, *Bible et vie chrétienne*, no. 62, 1965, 33-38.

(155). Principi della traduzione, *Rivista liturgica*, 52 (N.S. 1), 1965, 5-11. [See nos. 54 and 75.]

156. Problèmes de l'anaphore syrienne des apôtres Addaï et Mari, *L'Orient syrien*, 10, 1965, 89-106.

157. Les dénominations du dimanche dans la tradition chrétienne, in the collection: *Le dimanche* (Coll.: Lex orandi, 39), Paris, Éditions du Cerf, 1965, 7-28. [A lecture given in Paris, Saint-Serge, 1962.]

(158). A.-G. MARTIMORT, *L'Église en prière, 3ᵉ édition revue et corrigée*, Tournai et Paris, Desclée et Cie, 1965. [See no. 130. The text by Dom Botte is unchanged but the bibliography and the notes are brought up to date.] This revised edition has seen many translations:
A Igreja em oraçâo, Singeverga, Ediçôes Ora et Labora, 1965. See 17-39 and 40-50.
La Chiesa in preghiera, 2ª ed. riveduta e corretta sulla 3ª ed. originale, Rome, Desclée et Cie, 1966. See 16-36 and 37-47.
La Iglesia en oración, 2ª ed. revisada, Barcelona, Herder, 1967. See 41-60 and 61-70.
The Church at Prayer, New York, Desclée et Cie and Dublin, The Irish University Press, v. I, 1968; v. II, 1973. See I, 13-31 and 32-41. [In fact, this is a 4th edition, completely revised. The text by Dom Botte is unchanged, but the bibliography and notes are brought up to date.]

159. Tradition apostolique et canon romain, *La Maison-Dieu*, no. 87, 1966, 52-61.

160. A propos de la Tradition apostolique, *Recherches de théologie ancienne et médiévale*, 33, 1966, 177-186.

161. A propos de la confirmation, *Nouvelle revue théologique*, 88, 1966, 848-852. [See no. 162.]

(162). A proposito della confermazione, *Rivista liturgica*, 54 (N.S. 3), 1967, 103-109. Reprinted in the collection: *La confermazione et l'iniziazione cristiana* (Coll.: Quaderni di Rivista liturgica, 8), Turin, Elle Di Ci, 1967, 37-42. [Translation of no. 161.]

163. L'età della confermazione: riposta a Padre Cipriano Vagaggini, *La scuola cattolica*, 95, 1967, 270-274.

164. Maranatha, in the collection: *Noël, Épiphanie, retour du Christ* (Coll.: Lex orandi, 40), Paris, Éditions du Cerf, 1967, 25-42. [A lecture given in Paris, Saint-Serge, 1963.]

165. L'onction postbaptismale dans l'ancien patriarcat d'Antioche, *Miscellanea liturgica in onore di S.E. il Cardinale Giacomo Lercaro*, II, Rome, Desclée, 1967, 795-808.

166. In illo tempore, *Verbum caro*, 21, 1967, 71-77.

167. *Hippolyte de Rome. La Tradition apostolique, d'après les anciennes versions. Introduction, traduction et notes* (Coll.: Sources chrétiennes, 11 bis), Paris,

Éditions du Cerf, 1968. [A reedition of no. 36, entirely reworked according to no. 144.]

168. Art. Qui pridie, *Liturgisch Woordenboek*, 2, 1968, 2343-2344.

169. Mysterium fidei, *Bible et vie chrétienne*, no. 80, 1968, 29-34.

170. Où en est la réforme du canon de la messe?, *Les questions liturgiques et paroissiales*, 49, 1968, 138-141.

171. L'anaphore brève, *Anaphores*, Paris, Éditions du Cerf, 1968, 9-16.

172. Le nouveau rituel d'ordination, *Les questions liturgiques et paroissiales*, 49, 1968, 273-278. [See no. 173.]

(173). Het nieuwe wijdingsrituaal, *Tijdschrift voor liturgie*, 52, 1968, 388-393. [Translation of no. 172.]

174. Una cum famulo tuo Papa nostro, *Les questions liturgiques et paroissiales*, 49, 1968, 303-306.

175. Extendit manus suas cum pateretur, *Les questions liturgiques et paroissiales*, 49, 1968, 307-308.

(176). Extendit manus suas cum pateretur, *Tijdschrift voor liturgie*, 52, 1968, 451-453. [Translation of no. 175.]

177. Art. Supplice te rogamus, *Liturgisch Woordenboek*, 2, 1968, 2608.
Art. Supra quae, Ibidem, 2608-2609.
Art. Sursum corda, Ibidem, 2609.
Art. Te igitur, Ibidem, 2652.

178. Art. Prologues et sommaires de la Bible, *Dictionnaire de la Bible, Supplément*, 8, fasc. 44, 1969, 688-692.

179. L'ordination de l'évêque, *La Maison-Dieu*, no. 98, 1969, 113-126.

180. Vers une nouvelle édition du Missel romain, *Les questions liturgiques et paroissiales*, 50, 1969, 90-94. [See no. 181.]

(181). De nieuwe uitgave van het Missale Romanum onderweg, *Tijdschrift voor liturgie*, 53, 1969, 333-336. [Translation of no. 180.]

182. Apostolici reverentia culminis, *Au service de la Parole de Dieu. Mélanges offerts à Mgr André-Marie Charue, Évêque de Namur*, Gembloux, Duculot, 1969, 123-128.

183. Naar aanleiding van het wijdingsritueel, *Tijdschrift voor liturgie*, 54, 1970, 264-266.

184. Mortem tuam annuntiamus, *Tijdschrift voor liturgie*, 54, 1970, 398.

185. Les anaphores syriennes orientales, in the collection: *Eucharisties d'Orient et d'Occident* (Coll.: Lex orandi, 46 and 47), Paris, Éditions du Cerf, 1970, 2 vol., II, 7-24. [A lecture given in Paris, Saint-Serge, 1965.] See also the Introduction, 7-10.

186. Les traductions liturgiques de l'Écriture, in the collection: *La Parole dans la liturgie* (Coll.: Lex orandi, 48), Paris, Éditions du Cerf, 1970, 81-105. [A lecture given in Paris, Saint-Serge, 1966.] See also the Introduction, 7-8.

187. A propos des ordres mineurs, *Questions liturgiques*, 51, 1970, 129-132.

188. Sacrificium vivum, *Didaskalia*, 1, 1971, 5-9.

189. Problèmes de la confirmation, *Questions liturgiques*, 53, 1972, 3-8.

190. Deux passages de Tertullien: De baptismo 7, 1 et 8, 2, *Epektasis. Mélanges patristiques offerts au Cardinal Jean Daniélou*, Paris, Beauchesne, 1972, 15-18.

191. Communion eucharistique et communion des saints, *Questions liturgiques*, 53, 1972, fasc. 3-4. [A lecture given in Paris, Saint-Serge, 1972. See no. 193.]

(192). *La Tradition apostolique de saint Hippolyte. Essai de reconstitution* (Coll.: Liturgiewissenschaftliche Quellen und Forschungen, 39), Münster/ Westf., Aschendorff, 1972. [Fourth printing of no. 144, with 2 pages (III-IV) of Corrigenda et Addenda.]

(193). Communion eucharistique et communion des saints, *Présence orthodoxe*, 4, 1973, nos. 20-21, 47-55. [A reprint of no. 191.]

(194). Gemeinschaft der Eucharistie und Gemeinschaft der Heiligen, *Erbe und Auftrag*, 49, 1973, 299-308. [German translation of no. 191.]

195. *Le mouvement liturgique. Témoignage et souvenirs*, Tournai, Desclée, 1973. [In memory of Dom Lambert Beauduin on the occasion of the hundreth anniversary of his birth (4 August, 1873).]

196. Le pardon des péchés dans le Psautier, *Questions liturgiques*, 54, 1973, 181-190. [A lecture given in Paris, Saint-Serge, 1973. See nos. 197 and 208.]

(197). O perdão dos pecados no Saltério, *Ora et labora*, 20, 1973, 291-302. [Portugese translation of no. 196.]

198. Vatican II et le renouveau liturgique, *Au coeur de l'Afrique*, 6, 1974, 301-324. [See no. 199.]

(199). Vatican II and the Renovation of the Liturgy, in the collection: *Fides et theologia*. Dissertationes a pluribus theologia peritis exaratas doctrinam fidei et morum Ecclesia ... exponentes ... collegerunt et edierunt L. EL-DERS S.V.D., H. VAN STRAELEN S.V.D., Tokyo, Chuo Shuppansha (= Catholic Press Center), 1974, 403-435. [In Japanese; see no. 198.]

200. La libre composition des prières liturgiques, *Questions liturgiques*, 55, 1974, 211-215. [See no. 202.]

201. La vingt-et-unième Semaine de Saint-Serge (Paris, 1-5 juillet 1974), *Revue théologique de Louvain*, 5, 1974, 518-519.

202. La libre composition des prières liturgiques. Note rectificative, *Questions liturgiques*, 56, 1975, 60. [See no. 200.]

(203). Riso e tè per l'eucharistia?, *Liturgia*, 9, 1975, 244-245. [An extract, translated into Italian, of no. 142.]

204. Le traité des charismes dans les "Constitutions apostoliques," in the collection: *Studia patristica* XII (Coll: Texte und Untersuchungen zur Geschichte der altchristlichen Literatur, 115), Berlin, Akademie-Verlag, 1975, 83-86. [A communication sent to the VI Patristic Congress at Oxford, September, 1971.]

205. Ooikonomia. Quelques emplois spécifiquement chrétiens, in the collection: *Corona gratiarum. Miscellanea* ... *Eligio Dekkers* ... *oblata* (Coll.: Instrumenta patristica, 10), vol. I, Brugge, Sint-Pietersabdij en 's Gravenhange, Martinus Nijhof, 1975, 3-9.

206. Quelques souvenirs, in the collection: B. FISCHER - H.B. MEYER, *J.A. Jungmann. Ein Leben für Liturgie und Kerygma*, Innsbruck-Vienna-Munich, Tyrolia-Verlag, 1975, 24-25.

207. Les plus anciennes formules de prières pour les morts, in the collection: *La maladie et la mort du chrétien dans la liturgie* (Coll.: Bibliotheca "Ephe-

merides liturgicae. Subsidia", 1) Rome, Edizioni liturgiche, 1975, 83-99. [A lecture given in Paris, Saint-Serge, 1974.]

208. Le pardon des péchés dans le Psautier, in the collection: *Liturgie et rémission des péchés* (Coll.: Bibliotheca "Ephemerides liturgicae. Subsidia", 3), Rome, Edizioni liturgiche, 1975, 57-68. [See nos. 196 and 197.]

209. C. VOGEL, *Introduction aux sources de l'histoire du culte chrétien au moyen âge. Réédition anastatique préfacée par Bernard Botte* (Coll.: Biblioteca degli "Studi medievali", 1), Spoleto, Centro italiano di studi sull'Alto Medioevo, 1975, V-VI.

210. Die Wendung "astare coram et tibi ministrare" im Eucharistischen Hochgebet II, *Bibel und Liturgie*, 49, 1976, 101-104. [Presented to Msgr. Lengeling on the occasion of his 60th birthday.]

211. Les liturgies locales dans l'antiquité chrétienne, in the collection: *Liturgie de l'Église particulière et liturgie de l'Église universelle* (Coll.: Bibliotheca "Ephemerides liturgicae. Subsidia", 7), Rome, Edizioni liturgiche, 1976, 9-10. [Saint-Serge, Paris, 1975.]

212. La liturgie de Vatican II. Une mise au point du R.P. Botte, *La Libre Belgique*, 25 August, 1976, 1 and 5. [In regard to Archbishop Lefebvre.]

213. La vingt-troisième Semaine de Saint-Serge (Paris, 28 juin-1er juillet 1976), *Revue théologique de Louvain* 8, 1977, 105.

214. Art. Quentin (Dom Henri), *Dictionnaire de la Bible, Supplément,* 9, fasc. 50 B, 1977, 691-693.

215. Les débuts de l'emploi du microfilm pour l'étude des manuscrits, in the collection: *Studia codiologica* [= Festschrift Marcel Richard], (Coll.: Texte und Untersuchungen zur Geschichte der altchristlichen Literatur, 124), Berlin, Akademie-Verlag, 1977, 109-111. [See no. 218.]

216. A propos de la confirmation, *Questions liturgiques,* 58, 1977, 171-172.

217. Peuple chrétien et hiérarchie dans la "Tradition apostolique" de saint Hippolyte, in the collection: *L'assemblée liturgique et les différents rôles dans l'assemblée* (Coll.: Bibliotheca "Ephemerides liturgicae. Subsidia", 9), Rome: Edizioni liturgiche, 1977, 79-91. [Conférence de Saint-Serge, Paris 1976. See no. 228.]

(218). Wanneer en hoe men is begonnen de microfilm te gebruiken voor het bestuderen van handschriften, *Loven boven,* 1977-1978, no. 3, 23-27. [Dutch translation of no. 215.]

219. "Et elevatis oculis in caelum." Étude sur les récits liturgiques de la dernière Cène, in the collection: *Gestes et paroles dans les diverses familles liturgiques* (Coll.: Bibliotheca "Ephemerides liturgicae. Subsidia", 14), Rome, Centro liturgico Vincenziano, 1978, 77-86. [Conférence de Saint-Serge, Paris, 1977.]

(220). *O movimento litúrgico. Testemunho e recodações* (Coll.: Igreja-Eucaristia, 6), São Paulo, Ediçoes Paulinas, 1978. [Portuguese translation of no. 195, by D. Clemente ISNARD O.S.B.]

(221). Les conférences de Saint-Serge, *Nouvelles de Saint Serge,* 3, 1978, 5-8. [Extract of no. 195.]

222. Le vingt-cinquième anniversaire des Conférences Saint-Serge de Paris (27-30 juin 1978), *Questions liturgiques,* 59, 1978, 221-226.

223. La liturgie expression et gardienne de la foi. Un témoignage, in the collec-

tion: *La liturgie expression de la foi* (Coll.: Bibliotheca "Ephemerides liturgicae. Subsidia", 16), Rome, Centro liturgico Vincenziano—Edizioni liturgiche, 1979, 69-74. [Conférence de Saint-Serge, Paris, 1978. See no. 224.]

(224). De liturgie uitdrukking en bewaakster van het geloof. Een getuigenis, *Loven boven*, 1978-1979, no. 1, 9-14. [Dutch translation of no. 223.]

225. E. LODI, *Enchiridion euchologicum fontium liturgicorum*, (Coll.: Bibliotheca "Ephemerides liturgicae. Subsidia", 15), Rome: Edizioni liturgiche, 1979. Introduction by Bernard Botte, p. VII-VIII.

226. *Sapientiae doctrina*. Mélanges de théologie et de litterature médiévales offerts à dom Hildebrand Bascour O.S.B. (Recherches de théologie ancienne et médiévale, Special issue I), Louvain, 1979. Address by B. Botte, p. IX-XI.

(227). Christian People and Hierarchy in the "Apostolic Tradition" of St. Hippolytus, in the collection: *Roles in the Liturgical Assembly*, New York, Pueblo, 1981, 61-72. [See no. 217.]

Index of Proper Names